The Tequila Cook Book

by

Lynn Nusom

GOLDEN WEST ☼ PUBLISHERS

Cover illustration by Kris Steele
Interior art by Steve Parker and Jim Tutwiler

Library of Congress Cataloging-in-Publication Data
Nusom, Lynn.
  The Tequila Cook Book / by Lynn Nusom
      p.   cm.
  Includes index.
  ISBN 0-914846-89-2: $7.95
  1. Cookery (Tequila)   I. Title
TX726-N87 1993   93-21428
641.6'25--dc20   CIP

Printed in the United States of America

4th Printing © 2000

ISBN #0-914846-89-2

Golden West Publishers
4113 N. Longview Ave.
Phoenix, AZ 85014, USA
(602) 265-4392

Visit our website: Goldenwestpublishers.com

CONTENTS

Chicken Dishes

Fish & Seafood

Meat Dishes

Vegetable Dishes

Salsas & Sauces

Breads

Desserts

Beverages

INTRODUCTION

Why Tequila ?

When I told people I was working on a tequila cookbook—although they were most often too polite to verbalize the question I would get this quizzical look that asked "Why?"

For years cooks and chefs have found great delight in enhancing their cooking with all manner of alcoholic beverages; beer, wines in all hues, whiskeys, liqueurs from the very sweet to the medicinal tasting. But tequila has been, for the most part, overlooked as an ingredient in most cooking and it was only by accident that I discovered just how good it could be.

Several years ago while first experiencing the delights of the southwest and Mexico I naturally experimented with drinking tequila. It wasn't however, until much later, when we lived in Tucson that I started cooking with it.

One evening I'd invited a few people over for dinner. The main course called for sherry but there wasn't any in the house. So, I thought I'd substitute white wine or vermouth but—there again we'd run out of both. Since it was late and I was lazy I rummaged through the liquor cabinet discarding the Christmas brandy or any of the liqueurs like Chartreuse and Benedictine that one buys and that never seems to get used.

Then I spied the tequila bottle. After all, I said to myself, it is a clear liquid, and I removed the cap and smelled the contents. Interesting smell, albeit a little salty I thought. I had often used French vermouth a great deal in cooking and in a way the smell reminded me a little of it.

So, I said what 'ta hey—why not. I was in the southwest doing a regional dish—why not just go all the way. I added the tequila, served the meal and was rewarded for my daring with great praise.

Being a Leo and possessing a huge ego I thought I just might be onto something and continued to experiment with tequila in cooking from then on.

This book is a compilation of those recipes—collected, tried again, tested by friends and family—over the past twenty years.

What is Tequila?

Tequila is a distilled liquor made from one of 400 species of agave plant. This blue variety agave is successfully grown only in the Mexican state of Jalisco, and in portions of Michoacan and Nayart. The town of Tequila is in the latter, near Guadalajara.

People often think that tequila is a form of pulque or mescal—or vice versa. Although both of these liquors are made from agave they are not tequila unless they come from the BLUE agave.

The Mexican government has four tests that determine what is tequila. The first is that it is made from the juice of the blue agave. Secondly it must come from the areas mentioned above. The third qualifier is that the agave juice after fermentation must be distilled twice. The last rule is that the final product must contain at least fifty-one percent distilled agave juice and only forty-nine percent or less can be the result of distilled cane sugar.

There are many brands of tequila for sale in most liquor stores. There are also different colors of tequila. The white tequila is the most common and usually the least expensive. Gold tequila—called "especial" by some manufacturers is considered a premium tequila. The color is caused by aging the tequila in casks.

If you travel into Mexico, try different brands of tequila that are not readily available in the United States and use your liquor allotment to bring some back, as it is much less expensive than it is here.

Read on for more facts and lore about tequila as well as some delicious recipes you can make for yourself, family and friends.

Lynn Nusom

APPETIZERS

Tequila and the Blue Agave

The Spaniards had learned the fine art of the distillation of liquor in the sixteenth century and had become accustomed to enjoying strong drink. So it was only natural when they conquered Mexico that they look around for something to make liquor from.

They sampled the fermented beverage, called pulque, that the Indians made and found it lacking in strength compared to the distilled liquors they were used to. However, they decided that they would take the same juice from the agave plant (called mescal by the Indians) and try distilling it. They experimented until they discovered that the juice from the blue agave made the best tasting drink.

Tequila is still being distilled from the juice of the blue agave to this day, and modern man finds it just as pleasant tasting, and inebriating, as did those early Spanish settlers.

COCKTAIL MEATBALLS

Every time we serve these they're the first thing on the cocktail table or buffet to disappear.

1 EGG
1/2 cup TEQUILA
1 tsp. WORCESTERSHIRE SAUCE
1 Tbsp. fresh PARSLEY, chopped or 1 tsp. dried
1/2 tsp. CELERY SEED
1 tsp. RED CHILE POWDER
1 tsp. GROUND BLACK PEPPER
1 lb. GROUND BEEF
1 cup BREAD CRUMBS
1/2 cup PARMESAN CHEESE
3 - 4 Tbsp. CANOLA OIL

Whisk the egg with the tequila, worcestershire, parsley, celery seed, chile and pepper. Combine the mixture with the ground beef, bread crumbs and Parmesan cheese. Form the mixture into balls the size of a walnut. Heat the oil in a large frying pan and sauté the balls, turning gently to brown on all sides.

When cooked through, place on paper towels to drain and then serve with the **Chinese Style Dipping Sauce** (page 90) or your favorite barbecue sauce. *Serves 6 - 8.*

OLÉ SHRIMP DIP

2 cans (4 1/4 oz. each) SMALL SHRIMP, rinsed and drained
2 pkgs. (8 oz. each) CREAM CHEESE
1/4 cup SOUR CREAM
1/3 cup your favorite RED SALSA
1/4 cup TEQUILA
1 tsp. chopped CHIVES
1 Tbsp. fresh PARSLEY, finely chopped
1 Tbsp. fresh LIME JUICE

Mix all the ingredients together. Store in the refrigerator for at least two hours before serving. Serve with crackers or crudites. *Serves 6 - 8.*

BROCCOLI BALLS

Serve these at a cocktail party for your vegetarian friends.

Preheat oven to 400 degrees.

2 cups BROCCOLI, fresh or frozen, cooked and drained
1 carton (12 oz.) small curd COTTAGE CHEESE
1/2 cup grated PARMESAN CHEESE
1/2 cup BREAD CRUMBS
1/4 tsp. ground BLACK PEPPER
1/4 tsp. ground NUTMEG
2 EGGS, lightly beaten
1/2 cup TEQUILA
1/2 cup all-purpose FLOUR
1 Tbsp. PAPRIKA

Chop the broccoli and mix with the cottage cheese, Parmesan cheese, bread crumbs, pepper, nutmeg, eggs and tequila.   Form the mixture into balls approximately the size of walnuts, cover with plastic wrap and refrigerate overnight.   Mix the flour with the paprika in a shallow dish.   Roll the balls in the flour mixture and place on a cookie sheet that has been sprayed with non-stick cooking spray. Bake in a 400 degree oven for 10 - 15 minutes or until lightly browned and cooked through. *Serves 6 - 8.*

CHICKEN LIVER PATÉ

I've served this on two continents and although it's not "in" at the moment to eat organ meats, especially when they've been sautéed in butter—I still get great raves when I pass this dish around.

1/2 cup BUTTER
1/4 cup OLIVE OIL
1 lb. CHICKEN LIVERS
1/4 cup TEQUILA
1 Tbsp. PARSLEY, chopped

1/4 tsp. SALT
1/4 tsp. ground BLACK
    PEPPER
3 - 4 GREEN ONIONS

Melt the butter in a frying pan, add the oil and let heat.

Wash the chicken livers, and pat dry on paper towels. Sauté in the butter and oil until just cooked through. Do not overcook or the livers will be tough. Let cool for about 10 minutes. Spoon the livers into a blender or food processor with tequila, parsley, salt, pepper, and green onions. Process until smooth, spoon into a mold or bowl and refrigerate for 4 - 6 hours before serving. Serve with crackers, matzo or crudites. *Serves 6 - 8.*

VEGETABLE PATÉ

This delightful dish can be served on crackers or mounded on lettuce leaves with marinated artichoke hearts, olives, and celery sticks arranged around the paté for a nice starter for dinner instead of a green salad.

3 - 4 CARROTS
2 cups BROCCOLI
    FLORETS
2 cups CAULIFLOWER
    FLORETS
1/2 cup WALNUTS
2 Tbsp. TEQUILA

2 pkgs. (8 oz. each) CREAM
    CHEESE, (room temp.)
1 tsp. SAFFLOWERS
1/4 cup GREEN CHILE
1/2 tsp. CAYENNE
1 tsp. LEMON JUICE

Put the carrots, broccoli, cauliflower and walnuts in a food chopper or processor and chop very finely. Add the rest of the ingredients and process until smooth. Spoon into a decorative bowl and serve with your favorite crackers or pumpernickel bread. *Serves 6 - 8.*

MARINATED MUSHROOMS

1 **can (16 oz.) BUTTON MUSHROOMS** (The larger the mush
   rooms the better. If you can't find the large cans in you
   supermarket—try a food wholesaler or specialty food shops.)
1/2 cup OLIVE OIL
1/3 cup WHITE WINE VINEGAR
2 tsp. LEMON JUICE
1/2 cup TEQUILA
1 tsp. CURRY POWDER
1 Tbsp. CILANTRO, chopped

   Drain the mushrooms and spoon into a large glass bowl or
plastic container. Mix the rest of the ingredients and pour over the
mushrooms, stirring gently to make sure all the caps are coated
with the mixture. Refrigerate overnight before serving. Serve
garnished with sprigs of cilantro or parsley and toothpicks to spear
the mushrooms. *Serves 6 - 8.*

MARINATED OLIVES

*These are good served by themselves with drinks - or string two or
three on a toothpick and put into a dry tequila martini made with 2
ounces of tequila, and a sparse teaspoon of dry vermouth, stirred
over ice.*

1 cup LIME JUICE
1/2 cup ORANGE JUICE
1 cup TEQUILA
3 GARLIC CLOVES, run through a garlic press
1 LIME, unpeeled, sliced
1 ORANGE, unpeeled, sliced
2 cans (6 oz. each) PITTED BLACK
   RIPE OLIVES

   Mix together all the ingredients except the olives. Drain the
olives and place in a glass bowl or plastic container. Pour the
tequila mixture over the olives and refrigerate for at least 24 hours.
Drain off the liquid before serving. *Serves 6 - 8.*

IT'S A "GOTCHA!"

Don't tell anybody what's in this until AFTER they taste it. They're sure to be certain that peanut butter and red chile is not a good combination until after they've scarfed down half of it.

3 cups crunchy PEANUT BUTTER, with no sugar added
1/2 tsp. crushed RED CHILE such as pequin
2 Tbsp. LEMON JUICE
1/2 tsp. SOY SAUCE
1 tsp. PREPARED YELLOW MUSTARD
1/4 cup TEQUILA

Mix all the ingredients together in a food processor or blender. Serve with crudites. *Serves 6 - 8.*

CEVICHE

I know that most people come up with enchiladas, tacos and tortillas when asked what food first comes to mind when they think of Mexican cuisine. However, to my taste there is nothing more purely Mexican-tasting than ceviche. This dish is particularly good on a hot summer day, washed down with a cooling beverage made with tequila.

1/2 lb. small SCALLOPS
1/2 lb. BABY SHRIMP
1/2 cup LIME JUICE
1/2 cup TEQUILA
2 JALAPEÑOS, chopped
2 Tbsp. CILANTRO, chopped
1 RED BELL PEPPER, chopped

Toss all the ingredients together in a glass bowl, cover and chill in the refrigerator for at least 4 hours. Serve very cold on lettuce leaves with tortilla chips. *Serves 4 - 6.*

COLD EGGPLANT & GREEN CHILE APPETIZER

This is an adaptation of the great Italian dish, caponata. The green chile, cilantro and tequila make this a delightful southwestern dish, served on a bed of lettuce with crackers.

1 medium EGGPLANT (approx. 1 to 1 1/2 lbs.)
2 Tbsp. coarse (Kosher) SALT
4 Tbsp. OLIVE OIL
2 cloves GARLIC, run through a garlic press
1 medium ONION, chopped
2 ribs CELERY, chopped
1 tsp. CILANTRO, chopped
2 cups ripe TOMATOES,
     peeled and chopped
1/2 cup green CHILE, chopped
1/4 cup TEQUILA
1/2 cup BLACK OLIVES, sliced
2 Tbsp. CAPERS, drained
2 Tbsp. LIME JUICE
1 tsp. ground BLACK PEPPER
1 tsp. SALT

Peel and slice eggplant and place slices into a large bowl. Pour coarse salt over the eggplant, cover with cold water, weigh with a plate and let stand for 1/2 hour.   Drain, rinse under cold water, thoroughly dry on paper towels, and dice.

Heat the olive oil in a large heavy pot, and sauté the garlic, onion and celery for 3 - 4 minutes, add eggplant and cilantro and continue cooking for 5 - 6 more minutes. Stir in tomatoes, green chile and tequila and cook, over low heat until the eggplant is soft (about twenty minutes).   Remove from the heat, pour into a large bowl and let cool to room temperature.

Stir in olives, capers, lime juice, salt, and pepper and chill in the refrigerator at least an hour before serving. *Serves 6 - 8.*

SHRIMP COCKTAIL

I thought everyone knew how to make a shrimp cocktail until I had two people ask me at the same show how to do it. I wrote the recipe in the front of one of my books for each of them and then decided I'd better pass on some of my secrets for this simple but satisfying appetizer or first course.

You can use frozen shrimp, canned shrimp or cook your own.

If you buy "green" (uncooked) shrimp - put a whole lemon sliced in half, along with some commercial shrimp boil in water. Bring to a boil and then boil the shrimp for approximately 7 minutes or until they turn pink. Do not overcook or they will be tough. You can buy a good shrimp boil in most supermarkets.

To serve 4 people use **24 SHRIMP**

3 ribs CELERY, chopped

Divide the chopped celery in the bottom of shrimp cocktail bowls or stemmed glasses (for a picnic I use plastic glasses).

Arrange the shrimp on top of the sauce or, if they are large, hang them over the side of the bowl or glass.

COCKTAIL SAUCE:

1 cup CATSUP
2 Tbsp. PREPARED HORSERADISH—use more or less
     depending on how "hot" your horseradish is
2 tsp. LEMON JUICE
1 Tbsp. TEQUILA
LEMON WEDGES

Mix first four ingredients together and spoon the sauce equally over the shrimp and celery. Serve garnished with lemon wedges or slices.

SOUPS

A Longtime Favorite!

The Cuervo Gold® we used when testing some of these recipes reminded us of the long history of tequila. In 1795 the King of Spain issued the first license to produce tequila to Jose Maria Guadalupe Cuervo.

Another distillery was founded by Jose Maria Castaneda in the early 19th century. Cenobio Saugra purchased the plant in September 1873 and began exporting tequila to the United States. A century later there were a total of thirty-three distilleries in Mexico. A third of these were in the town of Tequila and produced approximately eighty percent of the total world's supply of tequila.

Most reports indicate that over ninety percent of the approximately forty million liters of tequila produced a year is exported to the United States. I don't know what computer genius factored it—but I also read that over six hundred million margaritas are consumed annually by thirsty folks from Augusta, Maine to Saint Augustine, Florida and from Manhattan to San Diego.

CREAM OF AVOCADO SOUP

We're mad for avocados served in all manner of dishes. If the avocados you buy at the supermarket aren't quite ripe, we find that putting them in a brown paper bag for a couple of days will speed the ripening process.

Another tip when using avocados is to sprinkle just a little lemon juice over them before proceeding with the recipe to help keep them from discoloring.

1 Tbsp. OLIVE OIL
1/2 ONION, finely chopped
4 medium, ripe AVOCADOS, peeled and pitted
2 tsp. LEMON JUICE
1/2 cup TEQUILA
1 can (14 1/2 oz.) CHICKEN BROTH
1/4 tsp. ground WHITE PEPPER
1 cup CREAM
2 Tbsp. fresh PARSLEY, chopped

    Sauté the onion in the olive oil until limp. Sprinkle the lemon juice over the avocados. Purée the avocados with the tequila and onion in a food processor or blender. Pour into a saucepan with the chicken broth and pepper and cook over medium high heat for 10 minutes. Stir in the cream and heat again until warmed through. Serve garnished with freshly chopped parsley. *Serves 4 - 6.*

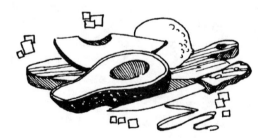

CONSOMMÉ CONSUELO

On my way to our test kitchen every day I pass a pastel portrait of Consuelo Vanderbilt. Reading menus from the era in which she lived, consommé always figures prominently, so although I doubt anyone served it to her with tequila - I decided to name this soup after her. However, my editor said the real reason for the name was that "consommé consuelo" was good alliteration.

3 cups LIGHT BEEF STOCK, strained, or 2 cans
   (14 1/2 oz. each) BEEF BROTH
1 cup TOMATO JUICE
2 Tbsp. LEMON JUICE
1/2 tsp. ground WHITE PEPPER
1 tsp. WORCESTERSHIRE SAUCE
1/2 cup TEQUILA
thinly sliced LEMON
fresh PARSLEY, finely chopped

   Stir together all of the ingredients, except lemon slices and parsley, in a saucepan and simmer over medium heat for 10 minutes or until warmed through. Dredge the lemon slices in the parsley and garnish the bowls of soup with them. *Serves 6 - 8.*

Agave Tequileana

Though there are four hundred species of plants called maguey, agave or century plant only the juice from the heart of a handful of these plants is made into mescal which usually has a sharp taste redolent of herbs. The blue agave or the agave tequileana is the only species of the maguey used to make tequila.

Tequila is the best known variety of mescal. It is named after a small town not far from Guadalajara in the Mexican state of Jalisco. Just as in France where only wines bottled in the Champagne region may be called champagne— Mexican law dictates that only mescal from the region around Guadalajara can be called tequila.

CORN CHOWDER

4 Tbsp. OLIVE OIL
1 ONION, chopped
2 cans (17 oz. each) CREAMED CORN
1/2 cup GREEN CHILE, chopped
1/4 cup TEQUILA
1/2 tsp. ground BLACK PEPPER
2 dashes TABASCO®
1 clove GARLIC, run through a garlic press
1 can (14 1/2 oz.) CHICKEN BROTH
1/2 cup CREAM or MILK

Heat the oil in a saucepan, add the onion and sauté until limp. Stir in the corn, chile, tequila, pepper, Tabasco, garlic, and chicken broth. Cook over low heat until warmed through, add the cream and continue cooking until hot - but do not let boil. *Serves 6 as a first course; serves 4 as a main course.*

SOPA DE CALABACITAS

(Squash Soup)

3 Tbsp. OLIVE OIL
1 ONION, chopped
4 medium SQUASH,
    zucchini or yellow
    crookneck, chopped
3 Tbsp. BUTTER
3 Tbsp. all-purpose FLOUR
1 cup MILK

3 cups CHICKEN STOCK
1/2 tsp. SALT
1/2 tsp. ground
    BLACK PEPPER
2 Tbsp. TEQUILA
1 cup CHICKEN, cooked,
    diced
sprigs of CILANTRO

Heat the oil in a large saucepan. Sauté onion and squash until onion is limp. Remove vegetables and reserve. Melt butter in the pan, stir in the flour to make a roux.   Add milk and cook, over medium heat, for 3 - 4 minutes, stirring occasionally. Stir in chicken stock. Add salt, pepper and squash and cook for 15 - 20 minutes. Stir in tequila and the chicken meat and cook for 5 - 10 minutes or until the chicken is warmed through. Serve garnished with cilantro *Serves 4.*

TOMATO SOUP FOR A WINTER'S NIGHT

This soup is perfect for those cold winter nights when you want something hot - but not a full meal. Perfect with toasted mozzarella cheese sandwiches.

1 can (28 oz.) CRUSHED
   TOMATOES
2 cups CHICKEN STOCK
   or BROTH
1/4 cup ORANGE JUICE
2 cloves GARLIC, pressed
1 tsp. ground SAGE

1 tsp. BASIL
1/2 tsp. ground BLACK
   PEPPER
1/2 tsp. SALT (optional)
1/4 cup TEQUILA
SOUR CREAM

Put tomatoes, chicken stock, orange juice, garlic, sage, and basil in a large saucepan and cook, over medium heat for 30 minutes, stirring two or three times during the cooking process.

Stir in pepper, salt and tequila and cook for 5 more minutes. Pour soup into heavy bowls or mugs, top with a dollop of sour cream and serve. *Serves 4.*

BLACK BEAN SOUP

1 lb. DRIED BLACK BEANS
WATER
2 Tbsp. OLIVE OIL
1 ONION, chopped
3 cloves GARLIC, minced
1 Tbsp. fresh PARSLEY or
   1 tsp. dried
2 CARROTS, diced

4 cups CHICKEN BROTH
   or STOCK
4 cups WATER
1/4 cup TEQUILA
3 Tbsp. SOUR CREAM
1/2 tsp. RED CHILE
   FLAKES

Pick the beans over and soak in water overnight. Rinse the beans the next day and hold. Heat the oil in a large soup pot, sauté the onion, garlic and parsley for 4 - 5 minutes. Add the beans, carrots, chicken broth, water, and tequila and cook for 3 hours or until beans are tender.

Pour hot soup into individual bowls. Mix sour cream and chile together, spoon a dollop on top of each bowl. *Serves 6 - 8.*

FARMERS MARKET SOUP

Although this soup is traditionally made with ground beef, it is also good made with half ground beef and half ground pork. A friend of ours also uses venison.

If you are trying not to eat red meat you can also make the meatballs with ground turkey or seafood, such as shrimp.

MEATBALLS:

6 Tbsp. OLIVE OIL
1 ONION, chopped
1 lb. GROUND BEEF
1/2 cup BREAD CRUMBS

1 Tbsp. dried PARSLEY
1/4 tsp. CUMIN
3 - 4 Tbsp. TEQUILA
1 EGG, lightly beaten

Heat 2 tablespoons of the olive oil in a frying pan and sauté onions until limp. Mix the cooked onions with the ground beef, bread crumbs, parsley, cumin, tequila and egg. Form the meat mixture into balls the size of a walnut and sauté in the remaining olive oil—gently turning to brown on all sides. When cooked through remove the balls to paper towels and reserve.

SOUP:

1 ONION, chopped
1/2 cup WATER
1 GREEN BELL PEPPER,
    chopped
6 RIBS CELERY, chopped
1/2 CABBAGE, chopped
1 SWEET POTATO, diced
1 can (30 oz.) WHITE
    HOMINY
2 cups PINTO BEANS

1 Tbsp. RED CHILE
    POWDER
1/2 tsp. dried OREGANO
6 cups WATER
1 can (14 oz.) BEEF
    BROTH
1 tsp. BLACK PEPPER
1 tsp. SALT (optional)
1/2 cup ORANGE JUICE
1/2 cup TEQUILA

Cook the onion, bell pepper and celery in 1/2 cup of water until limp. Combine the onion, bell pepper and celery with the rest of the ingredients in a large soup pot, cover and cook for 30 minutes. Add the meat balls and continue to cook for another 30 minutes.

CHEESE SOUP

The cooks of Mexico make extraordinary soups. This is my adaptation of one of the most wonderful soups served in many parts of Mexico.

1/4 cup OLIVE OIL
1 medium ONION, chopped
2 ribs CELERY, chopped
1 GREEN BELL PEPPER, chopped
1 can (14 1/2 oz.) CHICKEN BROTH
3 Tbsp. BUTTER
3 Tbsp. all-purpose FLOUR
1 qt. MILK
1/2 pint CREAM
1 cup VELVEETA® CHEESE, cubed
1/2 tsp. ground BLACK PEPPER
1/2 cup TEQUILA

Heat the oil in a saucepan and sauté the onion, celery and bell pepper for 6 - 7 minutes. Add the chicken broth and cook over medium heat for approximately 15 minutes or until the vegetables are tender.

Melt the butter in another pan and make a roux by adding the flour and stirring, then whisk in the milk and cream until the flour and butter are absorbed. Add the cheese and cook over low heat until melted. Add the chicken broth, vegetables, black pepper and tequila and simmer over very low heat for 15 minutes or until all the ingredients are blended together. Serve in bowls with crisp tortilla chips. *Serves 6 - 8.*

LAS VEGAS CHICKEN SOUP

This soup was not named for a gambler who went to Las Vegas, Nevada and could only afford chicken when he got home. Rather, it was named after the town in New Mexico where we first sampled its flavors.

1/2 lb. boneless, skinless CHICKEN BREASTS, diced
3 - 4 GREEN ONIONS, chopped
1 cup MUSHROOMS, sliced
1/4 cup TEQUILA
4 cups CHICKEN STOCK or BROTH
1/2 tsp. DRIED RED CHILE FLAKES (such as
      arbol or pequin)
4 cups WATER
1/2 head CABBAGE, shredded
2 CARROTS, diced
4 POTATOES, peeled, diced
1 Tbsp. fresh PARSLEY
1/2 tsp. ground BLACK PEPPER
1/4 tsp. ground GINGER

Put the chicken, mushrooms, tequila, 2 cups of water and red chile in a saucepan and cook for 30 minutes. Add the rest of the ingredients and cook for another 30 minutes. *Serves 6 - 8.*

Tequila si, Vino no!

Some things do not always translate literally from one language to another. A know-it-all friend of ours took us to a supper club in Mexico. Since he and his wife drink white wine he told the waiter that they would have "vino blanco-grandes."

Along with our lovely frosty margaritas the waiter delivered two large water tumblers full of clear liquid.

Not realizing that it was not white wine our friend took a large gulp and spit half of it out on the table. It was, of course, tequila since that is the common name in Mexico for any clear liquor. If our erstwhile friend had ordered "Vino de uva blanco" the waiter would have brought him the desired white wine.

HERMOSILLO ONION SOUP

The small city of Hermosillo in western Mexico is a very sophisticated metropolis with a university, superb artists and fine dining.

3 Tbsp. OLIVE OIL
2 Tbsp. NEW MEXICO RED CHILE POWDER
2 lg. YELLOW ONIONS, chopped
2 cans (14 1/2 oz. each) CHICKEN BROTH
1/4 cup TEQUILA
TOAST ROUNDS
1/2 cup GRUYERE CHEESE, shredded
1/4 cup ROMANO CHEESE, grated

Heat the oil in a large saucepan, stir in the chile powder and sauté onions for 10 minutes or until lightly browned. Add chicken broth, tequila and cook for 30 minutes over low heat. Pour into oven-proof soup dishes, top with a toast round, sprinkle with the gruyere and romano cheeses, place under a broiler until the cheeses melt. *Serves 4.*

CHILLED MUSHROOM– ASPARAGUS SOUP

2 Tbsp. OLIVE OIL
1/4 lb. MUSHROOMS, washed and sliced
1 lb. ASPARAGUS, large ends trimmed off, cooked
1 can (14 1/2 oz.) CHICKEN BROTH
2 cups MILK
1/3 cup TEQUILA
1/2 tsp. SALT
1/2 tsp. ground WHITE PEPPER
pinch NUTMEG
1 tsp. DILL WEED

Heat the oil in a frying pan and sauté the mushrooms until soft. Let cool and then purée in a food processor with the asparagus and the chicken broth. Pour into a saucepan and cook over medium high heat for 10 minutes. Stir in milk, tequila, salt, pepper, and nutmeg and continue cooking for another 5 minutes. Let cool and then chill in the refrigerator for two hours before serving. Garnish with dill and serve chilled. *Serves 4.*

GARLIC SOUP

This adaptation of a classic recipe is great for garlic lovers. I've also made converts to garlic by telling guests that a little of this soup before dinner will drive away evil spirits, cure a cold, and bring good luck—anything but start a romance.

4 WHOLE HEADS OF GARLIC, separated and peeled
6 Tbsp. BUTTER
4 Tbsp. OLIVE OIL
6 cups CHICKEN STOCK or BROTH
1/4 cup TEQUILA
1/2 tsp. ground BLACK PEPPER
1/2 tsp. SALT
1 Tbsp. fresh PARSLEY, chopped

Microwave each head of garlic for 30 seconds in the microwave on HIGH. This will make it easier to pop the garlic out of the shell. Heat the oil and melt the butter in a heavy saucepan, and sauté the garlic for 5 minutes or until it softens. Add the chicken stock and simmer for 20 minutes. Let cool slightly and blend in a blender. Return to the pan, add the rest of the ingredients and cook, over low heat, until warmed through. Makes a great lunch served with French bread, cheese and a green salad. *Serves 4 - 6.*

Olé!

When visiting Mexico many people think tequila is the fuel that fires the excitement which erupts into the word "olé." Although most often thought of as the substitution for "bravo" in the bullring—I think that when eating a particularly good dish a discreet "olé" is in order—especially if it has tequila in it.

BOUILLABAISSE

No self-respecting French chef would cook bouillabaisse this way—but living in the Southwest—the addition of the chile and the tequila came very naturally and gives this dish a fresh, new taste.

4 Tbsp. OLIVE OIL
1 WHITE ONION, chopped
2 cloves GARLIC, chopped
4 ribs CELERY, chopped
2 RED BELL PEPPERS, chopped
2 JALAPEÑOS, chopped
2 Tbsp. TOMATO PASTE
1/2 tsp. dried THYME
2 BAY LEAVES
8 cups FISH BROTH or CHICKEN BROTH
1/4 cup TEQUILA
1 tsp. TURMERIC
2 tsp. SAFFRON or SAFFLOWERS
1 lb. boneless RED SNAPPER fillets, cut into
    bite-size pieces
1 lb. boneless HALIBUT, cut into bite-size pieces
1 lb. large SHRIMP, peeled and deveined
1 doz. LITTLENECK CLAMS, well scrubbed
1 doz. MUSSELS, well scrubbed
1/4 cup fresh PARSLEY, chopped

Heat the oil in a large soup pot, stir in the onions and garlic, celery, red pepper and jalapeños. Cook for 3 - 4 minutes, then add tomato paste, thyme, bay leaves, broth, tequila, turmeric, and saffron. Cook for another 2 - 3 minutes then add the snapper and halibut and cook 2 minutes, add the shrimp, clams, mussels and parsley, bring to a rolling boil, cook for 5 - 7 minutes or until the shellfish is done. Discard the bay leaves and serve with French bread and a green salad. *Serves 6 - 8.*

SALADS

Piña and Aguamiel

The Mexicans have nicknamed the heart of the agave "piña" because its long, spike-shaped leaves bear a striking resemblance to a pineapple. The heart usually takes eight to ten years to mature and it reaches twenty to twenty-five inches in diameter. It will tip the scales at anywhere between eighty-five to one-hundred-fifty pounds. It is also interesting to note that the inside of the blue agave is a deep ivory when ripe.

At harvest time the leaves are chopped away from the heart and are shipped by truck to the distilleries. The piñas are then cut into smaller pieces, cooked, and the juice pressed out. The juice or syrup is called "aguamiel" which means "honey water" in English.

The syrup is then combined with cane sugar and yeast and left for forty-eight to fifty-two hours to ferment. A two-phase distillation process produces a tequila that is from one hundred to one hundred-ten proof. Distilled water is then added to make eighty and ninety percent proof tequila.

WILD RICE CHICKEN SALAD

2/3 cup uncooked WILD RICE
2 cups WATER
1 tsp. SALT
2 cups boneless, skinless, cooked,
    chopped white CHICKEN
1 Tbsp. fresh PARSLEY, chopped
4 - 5 GREEN ONIONS, chopped (include greens)
1 cup YELLOW PEAR TOMATOES, chopped
    (can substitute 2 medium-size red, ripe tomatoes,
    cut into eighths)
1/2 Tbsp. fresh MINT LEAVES, chopped
1/2 cup OLIVE OIL
1/4 cup GRAPEFRUIT JUICE
1/4 cup TEQUILA
1 tsp. SALT
1/2 tsp. ground BLACK PEPPER
WHOLE MINT LEAVES

Wash and rinse the wild rice. Cook the rice in 2 cups of water with the teaspoon of salt for 45 to 60 minutes or until rice is tender. Drain and let cool to room temperature. Place rice in a salad bowl with chicken, parsley, green onions, mint leaves and tomatoes.

Mix together olive oil, grapefruit juice, tequila, salt and pepper. Pour over salad, toss lightly, garnish with whole mint leaves and serve. *Serves 4 - 6.*

The Liquor with the Worm in it?

One of the best-selling mescals is bottled in a black, clay pot with a little pouch containing salt and ground up toasted worms from the maguey plant. Very often when talking about tequila the uninitiated will exclaim "Oh, yes the liquor with the worm in it." No, that is usually mescal and I've yet to see tequila with a worm in it for sale in this country, however tequila flavored lollipops with a worm in them are available throughout the Southwest.

MARY DUGGAN'S COLE SLAW

In the days before Tucson became a big city, Mrs. Duggan, an old friend of the family, made this spicy slaw for every potluck she went to. It was so good the people in the community made sure she was always invited.

3 cups shredded CABBAGE
2 cups shredded RED CABBAGE
2 CUCUMBERS, seeded and diced
4 - 5 GREEN ONIONS, chopped
2 GREEN BELL PEPPERS, chopped
1/2 cup SOUR CREAM
1/2 cup MAYONNAISE
1/4 cup TEQUILA
2 Tbsp. LEMON JUICE
1/2 tsp. DIJON MUSTARD
1/2 tsp. SALT
1 tsp. ground BLACK PEPPER
1 tsp. dried PEQUIN CHILE FLAKES

Put the cabbages, cucumber and bell peppers in a large salad bowl. Mix together the sour cream, mayonnaise, tequila, lemon juice, mustard, salt, pepper and chile and stir into the vegetables and refrigerate until ready to serve. *Serves 10 - 12.*

AVOCADO & WHITE BEAN SALAD

1 can (15 oz.) GARBANZO BEANS, drained
1/2 cup sliced BLACK OLIVES
1/2 cup OLIVE OIL
1/3 cup TEQUILA
2 Tbsp. LIME JUICE
1 tsp. CURRY POWDER
1 Tbsp. fresh or 1/2 tsp. dried BASIL
1/4 tsp. dried OREGANO LEAVES
CILANTRO AND PARSLEY for garnish
1 RED ONION, sliced
1/4 lb. HARD SALAMI, sliced into strips
3 ripe TOMATOES, cut into wedges
1 head of LEAF LETTUCE, washed, and dried
4 ripe AVOCADOS, sliced
1 Tbsp. LEMON JUICE

Mix all the ingredients except lettuce leaves, avocados and lemon juice together and let marinate in the refrigerator for 2 hours. Arrange lettuce leaves on individual salad plates, spoon the marinated salad onto the lettuce.   Sprinkle lemon juice over the avocado slices, and arrange them around the salad. Serve at once. *Serves 4 - 6.*

Añejo

Tequila may be drunk as soon as it is bottled since the juice matures in the plant. However, some tequila is aged in wine casks for one to seven years and is labeled "añejo" (aged).

ORANGE PECAN SALAD

1 clove GARLIC, peeled and cut in half
1 head RED LEAF LETTUCE, washed, dried
    and torn into bite size pieces
1/2 head ROMAINE LETTUCE, washed, dried
    and torn into bite size pieces
1 cup CELERY, chopped
3 - 4 GREEN ONIONS, chopped
1/2 cup PECANS, chopped
1 can (11 oz.) MANDARIN ORANGES
1/4 cup TEQUILA
1/4 cup OLIVE OIL
2 Tbsp. BALSAMIC VINEGAR

Rub the garlic halves into the sides and bottom of a salad bowl. Put the lettuces, celery, onions, pecans, and oranges in the bowl. Mix together the tequila, olive oil and vinegar, pour over the salad and toss. Serve at once. *Serves 4 - 6.*

SPINACH SALAD
WITH PECAN DRESSING

1 lb. SPINACH LEAVES (select young, tender leaves)
    washed and torn into bite-size pieces
2 AVOCADOS, peeled, sliced
1 RED ONION, sliced
3 Tbsp. OLIVE OIL
1 Tbsp. WHITE WINE VINEGAR
1/2 cup TEQUILA
1 Tbsp. LEMON JUICE
1/2 cup PECANS, chopped
1/2 tsp. RED CHILE FLAKES such as pequin or arbol

Place the spinach leaves, avocado slices and onion in a salad bowl. In a separate bowl, mix together oil, vinegar, tequila, lemon juice, pecans and chile. Pour the dressing over the salad and toss lightly. *Serves 4.*

SALPICON

This is my adaptation of a delightfully easy salad to make. It's a great way to use leftover roast beef.

1 cup ROAST BEEF, shredded
1/2 head LEAF LETTUCE, washed dried and torn into
   bite-size pieces
3 - 4 GREEN ONIONS, sliced
3 Tbsp. OLIVE OIL
3 Tbsp. TEQUILA
3 Tbsp. BALSAMIC VINEGAR
1 Tbsp. LIME JUICE
1 tsp. OREGANO

Place the roast beef, lettuce and onions in a salad bowl. Mix together oil, tequila, vinegar, lime juice and oregano. Pour the dressing over the salad, toss lightly and serve. *Serves 4.*

ONION & TOMATO SALAD

This is a great salad to make ahead while you grill meat or fish for dinner. It's also a nice salad to take to a potluck dinner.

2 cloves GARLIC, run through a garlic press
3 Tbsp. OLIVE OIL
1 Tbsp. WHITE WINE VINEGAR
1 tsp. DILL WEED, chopped
1 Tbsp. fresh PARSLEY, chopped
1 tsp. DIJON MUSTARD
2 Tbsp. TEQUILA
1/2 tsp. SALT
1/2 tsp. ground BLACK PEPPER
2 RED ONIONS, thinly sliced
4 - 5 TOMATOES, cut into wedges

Mix garlic, oil, vinegar, dill, parsley, mustard, tequila, salt, and pepper together in the bottom of a wooden salad bowl. Stir in onion and tomato and let stand at room temperature for 1/2 hour before serving. Stir again and serve. *Serves 4 - 6.*

"MAKE YOU PROUD" POTATO SALAD

We do a lot of catering. One of our long-time customers wanted a "country picnic" party and her husband said she had to have one of his favorite dishes—potato salad. She didn't think that was fancy enough to serve her guests but since he was footing the bill decided she'd better go with it. I said, "Don't worry. We'll give you a potato salad that'll make you proud."

2 lbs. WHITE POTATOES, peeled, boiled and diced
3 - 4 ribs CELERY, diced
CELERY TOPS, diced
4 - 5 GREEN ONIONS, diced (include greens)
1/2 cup BLACK OLIVES, pitted, sliced
1/2 cup GREEN OLIVES with pimentos, sliced
2 CUCUMBERS, peeled, seeded, diced
1 Tbsp. fresh CILANTRO or PARSLEY
1/2 cup SOUR CREAM
1/2 cup MAYONNAISE
1/4 cup TEQUILA
2 Tbsp. DIJON MUSTARD
1 Tbsp. LEMON JUICE
1 Tbsp. fresh DILL WEED (or 1 tsp. dried)
1/2 tsp. ground BLACK PEPPER
1/2 tsp. SALT
1 tsp. crushed RED PEPPER FLAKES (Pequin)

Put the potatoes, celery, celery tops, onions, olives, and cucumber in a large salad bowl. Add the rest of the ingredients and toss lightly. Garnish with sliced olives and sprigs of cilantro or parsley. *Serves 8 - 10.*

SUMMER PARTY SALAD

2 cloves GARLIC, cut in half
1 small head of CAULIFLOWER, broken into
    bite-size pieces
1 RED ONION, sliced
8 large MUSHROOMS, washed and sliced
1 GREEN BELL PEPPER, sliced
1 RED BELL PEPPER, sliced
1 YELLOW BELL PEPPER, sliced
1 cup BLACK OLIVES, sliced
1 head ICEBERG LETTUCE, washed and torn into
    bite-size pieces
1 head LEAF LETTUCE, washed and torn into
    bite-size pieces
3 Tbsp. OLIVE OIL
1/4 cup TEQUILA
2 Tbsp. LEMON JUICE
1 Tbsp. BALSAMIC VINEGAR
1 Tbsp. fresh PARSLEY, chopped
1 Tbsp. Fresh SWEET BASIL, chopped
1/2 tsp. OREGANO

Rub the sides of a salad bowl with the garlic, then run it through a garlic press and add to the dressing.

Put all the vegetables into a large salad bowl. In a separate bowl mix together oil, tequila, lemon juice, vinegar, parsley, basil and oregano, pour over the salad and toss lightly. *Serves 8 - 10.*

NAOMI'S FAVORITE GREEN SALAD

My aunt, Naomi Munson, introduced me to avocados when I was still a child. Although she served this salad with a strong blue cheese dressing the addition of the tequila is mine.

1 head ROMAINE LETTUCE, washed and torn into
    bite-size pieces
1 head LEAF LETTUCE such as BOSTON, BUTTER or
    RED LEAF, washed and torn into bite-size pieces
2 AVOCADOS, peeled, pitted and sliced
1 tsp. LEMON JUICE
1 RED ONION, sliced

    Place the lettuce in a large salad bowl. Pour the lemon juice over the avocado slices and add to the bowl. Top with red onion slices and **Signature Blue Cheese Dressing.** *Serves 4.*

SIGNATURE BLUE CHEESE DRESSING

1 cup MAYONNAISE
1/2 cup SOUR CREAM
1/2 tsp. ground BLACK PEPPER
1 Tbsp. fresh BASIL, torn into pieces
3 Tbsp. BLUE CHEESE
1 CUCUMBER, with the seeds scraped out,
    and finely chopped
1/4 cup TEQUILA

    Mix all the ingredients together, pour over salad.

ORANGE & CAULIFLOWER SALAD

3 ORANGES, peeled and sectioned
1/2 head CAULIFLOWER, broken into florets
1 GREEN BELL PEPPER, cut into rings
1 RED BELL PEPPER, cut into rings
1/2 RED ONION, sliced into rings

Place the oranges, cauliflower, bell peppers, and onion in a salad bowl. Toss with **Tequila Vinaigrette Dressing**.

TEQUILA VINAIGRETTE DRESSING

6 Tbsp. OLIVE OIL
3 Tbsp. TEQUILA
2 Tbsp. ORANGE JUICE
1/2 tsp. SALT
1/2 tsp. ground WHITE PEPPER
1 tsp. grated ORANGE PEEL
1/2 tsp. dried ROSEMARY

Mix together all ingredients. Pour over salad and toss lightly. *Serves 4 - 6.*

MUSTARD-HONEY SALAD DRESSING

We particularly like this dressing with a combination salad made with greens and fruit—such as spinach and mandarin oranges.

1/4 cup HONEY
2 Tbsp. DIJON MUSTARD
1/4 cup TEQUILA
3 Tbsp. OLIVE OIL
1/2 tsp. freshly ground BLACK PEPPER
1 clove GARLIC, run through a garlic press

Mix all the ingredients together. If you store it in the refrigerator be sure and let it come up to room temperature for at least an hour before using.

SUMMER FRUIT SALAD

Pat Healy, gift store owner, caterer, decorator, and florist is always coming up with new, inventive and tasty recipes. Here is one of his latest that he kindly gave me permission to pass on to you.

PURPLE KALE or another colorful, ruffled edge green
1 medium size CANTALOUPE, peeled, seeded and sliced
2 ORANGES, peeled and sectioned
1 pint STRAWBERRIES, hulled and sliced
1 pint BLACKBERRIES

Place the kale on four individual salad plates and arrange slices of cantaloupe, orange sections, strawberries and blackberries over the lettuce, then top with **Tequila-Yogurt Dressing**.

TEQUILA-YOGURT DRESSING

1 cup PLAIN YOGURT
1/2 cup MAYONNAISE
2 Tbsp. TEQUILA
2 Tbsp. HONEY
SPRIGS OF MINT

Mix all the ingredients together except the mint and pour over salad.   Garnish with sprigs of mint and serve.

ROSEMARY-TEQUILA CHICKEN SALAD IN PUFF PASTRY SHELLS

This makes a great dish for a summer luncheon.

2 WHOLE CHICKEN BREASTS, split and skinned
2 cups CHICKEN BROTH
1/4 cup TEQUILA
1 Tbsp. ROSEMARY, crushed
WATER

Put the chicken breasts in a large pan, with the chicken broth, tequila, rosemary and water to cover. Cook over medium heat for 30 minutes or until the chicken is tender. Let cool, then remove chicken meat from the bones and coarsely chop.

4 GREEN ONIONS, chopped (include greens)
1 CUCUMBER, peeled, seeded and diced
1 Tbsp. fresh PARSLEY, chopped
1/2 cup unsalted CASHEWS
1/4 cup MAYONNAISE
1/4 cup SOUR CREAM
1/2 tsp. ground WHITE PEPPER
1/4 tsp. SALT
1 Tbsp. TEQUILA

Mix all the ingredients together, place in refrigerator and chill while preparing the pastry.

8 large PUFF PASTRY SHELLS or your favorite
**   puff pastry recipe**

Prick the pastry shells with the tines of a fork and bake in a 350 degree oven for 10 minutes or until the pastry shells are lightly browned. Let cool, then fill with the chicken salad, garnish with springs of cilantro or parsley. *Serves 8.*

SHRIMP & PASTA SALAD WITH TEQUILA CHILE DRESSING

1 lb. PASTA such as Bow Ties, Circles, Stars or Elbows
    cooked according to package directions, drained and
    chilled in the refrigerator.
2 cans (4 1/2 oz. each) BABY SHRIMP, drained
1/2 LEMON
1 medium size CUCUMBER, seeded and diced
3 - 4 ribs CELERY, chopped
3 - 4 GREEN ONIONS, chopped
1 Tbsp. fresh PARSLEY, chopped
1/2 cup MAYONNAISE
1/2 cup SOUR CREAM
2 Tbsp. TEQUILA
1/2 tsp. DRIED RED CHILE FLAKES
1/2 tsp. SALT
1/2 tsp. ground BLACK PEPPER
1 tsp. dried CHIVES
JUICE OF HALF A LEMON
RED BELL PEPPER RINGS
GREEN BELL PEPPER RINGS

Put the chilled pasta in a salad bowl. Squeeze the 1/2 lemon
over the shrimp, and add to the pasta. Stir in the cucumber, celery,
onions and parsley. Mix together the mayonnaise, sour cream,
tequila, red chile flakes, salt, pepper, chives and lemon juice. Stir
well, pour over the pasta salad, toss and serve garnished with red
and green bell pepper rings. *Serves 6 - 8.*

CHICKEN DISHES

Tequila . . . Purely Medicinal?

As my maternal grandmother used to say with a twinkle in her eye when she took a sip of whiskey once in a while; "this is purely for medicinal purposes."

There are a lot of people who claim that drinking tequila is good medicine for both body and soul, and the heart of the agave has been used as a nutritious food source since the days of the Aztecs.

Many people take the old Mexican adage, "Para todo mal mescal, y para todo bien también" (mescal is a remedy for everything bad, and to celebrate all good as well) to heart and feel that tequila can purify the blood, disinfect a cut or cure dysentery. I have also heard the claim that along with olives, and certain types of mushrooms, tequila is a remarkable aphrodisiac.

An English friend of mine travels with a small flask of tequila in case of sunstroke and one of our neighbors claims that he has reached the venerable age of ninety-two by faithfully drinking two glasses of tequila a day—through two world wars, three marriages and a trip to New York.

CHICKEN BREASTS WITH ORANGE HOLLANDAISE SAUCE

I know, I know—hollandaise is fattening and uses artery-clogging eggs and butter. If anyone tells you it's a no-no just say that you need to get your vitamin C—so it's all right.

Preheat oven to 375 degrees.

4 WHOLE CHICKEN BREASTS
4 Tbsp. OLIVE OIL
1 tsp. PAPRIKA or NEW MEXICO RED CHILE POWDER
1 Tbsp. fresh PARSLEY, chopped or 1 tsp. dried
2 cloves GARLIC, run through a garlic press
1/2 cup TEQUILA
1/4 cup ORANGE JUICE
1/2 cup WATER

Soak the chicken breasts in lightly salted water for 1/2 hour. Drain and pat dry on paper towels and place in a baking dish. Mix together oil, paprika, parsley, garlic, tequila, orange juice and water and pour over chicken breasts. Bake in a 375 degree oven for 30 - 45 minutes, basting occasionally, until the chicken breasts are done. Serve with **Orange Hollandaise Sauce**. *Serves 4.*

ORANGE HOLLANDAISE SAUCE

3 EGG YOLKS
1 Tbsp. undiluted frozen
   ORANGE JUICE
1 Tbsp. GOLD TEQUILA

2 Tbsp. COLD BUTTER
1 cup MELTED BUTTER
dash SALT

Beat the eggs and pour in a heavy saucepan. Beat orange juice and tequila into egg yolks. Put over low heat and whisk 1 tablespoon of butter into egg mixture. Remove from the heat and whisk in the second tablespoon of cold butter. Then whisk in the melted butter, adding it in a steady, slow stream. Stir in the salt and whisk until the mixture is thick and creamy.

CHICKEN CASHEW

Although rice wine and sherry are most often used in Chinese cooking, I find tequila gives this stir-fry dish a lovely, unique flavor.

1/2 to 3/4 lb. CHICKEN BREASTS, boned, skin removed, thinly sliced
1/4 cup TEQUILA
1 tsp. RED CHILE FLAKES
3 Tbsp. PEANUT OIL
2 cloves GARLIC, minced
1/4 lb. MUSHROOMS, washed, sliced
1/4 lb. SNOW PEAS, washed
1/2 cup UNSALTED CASHEWS, chopped
1 Tbsp. fresh PARSLEY
1/2 tsp. ground BLACK PEPPER
1 tsp. SESAME OIL
1/2 tsp. LIGHT SOY SAUCE

Marinate the chicken in the tequila and chile for 1/2 hour. Dry the chicken on paper towels. Heat 2 Tbsp. of the oil in a wok or heavy frying pan. Stir in garlic and chicken breasts and stir fry for 4 - 5 minutes or until the chicken is done. Remove chicken with a slotted spoon to a warm platter and keep warm. Add the rest of the oil and stir fry mushrooms and snow peas for 3 - 4 minutes or until the mushrooms are just tender. Add chicken back to the wok with cashews, parsley, salt, pepper, sesame oil and soy sauce. Stir fry for 1 - 2 minutes or until everything is hot. Serve with rice or oriental noodles. *Serves 2.*

CHICKEN CURRY

This is a great way to use leftover chicken. The amount of curry you add depends on how hot you like your food. I recently was demonstrating a hot chile dish at a show when a group of English visitors stopped by. Their American host warned them that a taste of my chile might be too hot for them. They laughed and said that anyone who frequented the Indian restaurants in the Soho section of London and liked curry could stand anything dished up in the Southwest.

1 ONION, chopped
3 Tbsp. OLIVE OIL
2 Tbsp. all-purpose FLOUR
1 cup MILK
1 can (14 1/2 oz.) CHICKEN BROTH
1/4 cup TEQUILA
1 to 3 tsp. CURRY POWDER
2 cups CHICKEN BREASTS, cooked, diced
1 cup RAISINS
1 cup PINEAPPLE CHUNKS

Heat 2 tablespoons of the oil in a large saucepan and sauté the onions until limp. Remove onions with a slotted spoon and reserve. Add the remaining oil and stir the flour into it to make a roux. Stir in the milk, chicken broth, tequila and curry and cook, over medium heat, until the mixture thickens slightly. Add chicken, raisins, and pineapple. Cook over medium heat until all the ingredients are warmed through. Serve over rice with bowls of finely chopped peanuts, coconut, and chutneys such as **Tequila Chutney** (see next page) to sprinkle over the top of the curry. *Serves 4.*

TEQUILA CHUTNEY

Chutneys, of course, can be made of all sorts of things: green tomatoes, pears, mangoes and berries. I like this simple apple one and use Granny Smith apples if I can get them.

3 medium size APPLES,   1 Tbsp. CHIVES, chopped
   cored and diced   1/4 cup TEQUILA
JUICE OF ONE LIME   pinch SALT
1/2 cup RAISINS
2 Tbsp. PRESERVED GINGER, diced

Mix apples and lime juice together, then stir in the rest of the ingredients, cover and refrigerate for at least 4 hours before using. Great with curry dishes or served on the side with roast beef or pork. *Serves 4.*

TEQUILA & DIJON MARINATED CHICKEN BREASTS

4 CHICKEN BREASTS, boneless and skinless
1 Tbsp. coarse (Kosher) SALT
1/4 cup TEQUILA
3 Tbsp. DIJON MUSTARD
3 GREEN ONIONS, chopped (include greens)
1/4 cup OLIVE OIL
1 Tbsp. LEMON JUICE
1 clove GARLIC, cut in half

Soak the chicken breasts in water to cover with the tablespoon of salt.   Drain and rinse under cold running water and place in a glass dish or bowl.   Mix together the rest of the ingredients and pour over chicken breasts.   Cover with plastic wrap and marinate in the refrigerator for 4 hours.

Remove chicken from marinade and grill over hot coals for approximately 20 minutes, turning and basting with the marinade occasionally.   Discard any leftover marinade. *Serves 4.*

LEMON-TARRAGON BARBECUED CHICKEN

2 frying CHICKENS, cut in half
3 Tbsp. coarse (Kosher) SALT
WATER
1 Tbsp. dried TARRAGON
1 tsp. LEMON PEEL

1/3 cup LEMON JUICE
1/2 cup TEQUILA
1/2 cup OLIVE OIL
2 Tbsp. JALAPEÑOS, sliced

Soak chicken in salt and water to cover for 30 minutes. Rinse under cold water and pat dry with paper towels. Place in a shallow dish. Mix together tarragon, lemon peel, lemon juice, tequila, oil and jalapeños and pour over the chicken. Marinate for 2 hours then cook the chicken over a barbecue or broil, brushing occasionally with the marinade. Discard marinade when through cooking. *Serves 4.*

SUNDAY MORNING CHICKEN LIVERS

Chicken livers for breakfast on a quiet Sunday or holiday are just wonderful. I used to do these with red wine but have found that the tequila gives the livers a depth of flavor that the wine doesn't. These are also great served for a late night after-the-show supper.

1 lb. CHICKEN LIVERS, washed
   with the membranes removed
MILK

4 Tbsp. OLIVE OIL
6 Tbsp. BUTTER
1/2 cup TEQUILA

Soak chicken livers in milk to cover for 1/2 hour. Drain and pat dry on paper towels. Heat oil and butter in a frying pan. Sauté chicken livers for 5 - 7 minutes over medium high heat until livers are just pink inside or done to taste. Remove to a warm platter. Deglaze the pan with the tequila, pour over chicken livers and serve with scrambled eggs and English muffins. *Serves 4 - 6.*

COQ AU TEQUILA

We've enjoyed coq au vin for a long time—but lately have tired of the heavy red wine taste. This method using the tequila makes for a lighter, more modern taste.

2 medium CHICKENS, cut into serving pieces
WATER
2 Tbsp. coarse (Kosher) SALT
1 cup all-purpose FLOUR
1 tsp. ground BLACK PEPPER
1 tsp. NEW MEXICO RED CHILE FLAKES or
     2 tsp. PAPRIKA
1/4 cup plus 3 Tbsp. OLIVE OIL
1/4 cup BRANDY
1 can (12 oz.) V8® JUICE
2 cups TEQUILA
1 cup WATER
3 ONIONS, quartered
16 - 20 MUSHROOM CAPS

Soak chicken in water to cover with salt for 1/2 hour.   Rinse under cold running water and pat dry with paper towels. Put flour, pepper and chile into a paper sack or plastic bag and shake the chicken pieces to coat them.   Heat 1/4 cup of oil in a heavy Dutch oven and brown the chicken. Warm brandy, pour it over the chicken and ignite it.   When the flame has died down, add the V8, tequila and water and cook, over medium heat, for 45 minutes or until the chicken is tender.

In a frying pan heat remaining oil and sauté onion quarters for 5 - 7 minutes, add the mushroom caps and continue cooking until mushrooms are tender.   Arrange cooked chicken on a platter, arrange onions and mushrooms around it, ladle some of the sauce* over it and serve at once.

* If the sauce is not thick enough to your taste - make a roux with 2 Tbsp. of butter and 2 Tbsp. of all-purpose flour, and stir the liquid from chicken into the roux. Reduce the heat and cook for 3 - 4 minutes, whisking occasionally.   Serve over the chicken. *Serves 4 - 6.*

MARGARITA CHICKEN PEQUIN

This is one of my favorite dishes and I have demonstrated it at shows around the country including the Fiery Food Fair in Albuquerque. It gets thumbs-up approval every time.

4 Tbsp. all-purpose FLOUR
1 tsp. crushed PEQUIN CHILE
1/3 tsp. OREGANO
4 boneless, skinless CHICKEN BREASTS
4 Tbsp. OLIVE OIL
2 cloves GARLIC, run through a garlic press
4 Tbsp. TEQUILA
2 Tbsp. TRIPLE SEC

4 Tbsp. LIME JUICE
1 tsp. crushed PEQUIN CHILE
1/2 tsp. coarse (Kosher) SALT
1 Tbsp. BUTTER
2 - 3 GREEN ONIONS, chopped
Sprigs of CILANTRO
LIME slices
2 - 3 whole PEQUIN CHILE PEPPERS that have been marinated in olive oil*

Mix the flour, the first teaspoon crushed pequin chile and the oregano together in a shallow dish. Dredge the chicken breasts in the mixture. Heat the oil in a large frying pan, stir in the garlic and then sauté the chicken breasts until done (approximately 10 - 15 minutes). While the chicken is cooking mix together the tequila, triple sec, lime juice and salt. When the chicken breasts are done, remove to a warm plate and keep warm.

Pour the tequila mixture into the pan and stir to deglaze the pan. Add the second teaspoon of pequin chile and cook over high heat until the mixture is reduced and slightly thickened. Stir in the butter, cook for about a minute longer and pour over the chicken breasts. Sprinkle the top with the chopped green onion, garnish with the cilantro sprigs and lime slices and one or two whole pequins and serve. *Serves 4.*

*You can use this oil in place of plain olive oil to sauté the chicken in for a hotter taste.

HOMINY-RED CHILE CHICKEN BURRITO

The humble burrito—originally designed as a simple, easy to carry lunch—goes uptown with this recipe.

2 Tbsp. OLIVE OIL
1/2 ONION, diced
1 clove GARLIC, minced
1 cup CHICKEN BREAST,
    cooked, chopped
2 cups WHITE HOMINY
1 cup RED CHILE SAUCE

1 Tbsp. FRESH CILANTRO
1/2 tsp. dried OREGANO
1/2 tsp. ground CUMIN
1 Tbsp. TEQUILA
JUICE OF 1 LIME
6 - 8 FLOUR TORTILLAS

Heat olive oil in a frying pan and sauté the onion for 5 minutes. Add garlic, chicken breast, hominy, red chile sauce, cilantro, oregano, cumin and tequila and cook until warmed through. Stir in lime juice and spoon onto warm flour tortillas. Roll tortilla up and serve with refried black beans and rice. *Serves 4.*

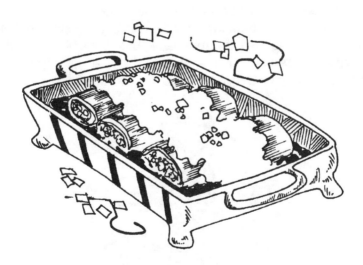

GRILLED ORANGE
& TEQUILA CHICKEN

This is a very simple dish—takes a little preplanning, however. I find it works best to put the chicken in the marinade in the morning and grill it for dinner.

4 CHICKEN BREASTS, skinless, boneless
4 GREEN ONIONS, chopped
1/2 cup ORANGE JUICE
1/2 cup TEQUILA
1/4 cup LEMON JUICE
1 tsp. grated ORANGE RIND
1 JALAPEÑO

Place chicken breasts in a shallow dish. Sprinkle the chopped onions over chicken. Mix together orange juice, tequila, lemon juice, orange rind and jalapeño. Pour the mixture over the chicken, cover and refrigerate for 6 - 8 hours, turning two or three times during the day.

Remove the chicken from the marinade, let stand at room temperature for 1/2 hour then grill over hot coals approximately 20 minutes, basting with the marinade, until the chicken is done. Discard any remaining marinade and serve the chicken with polenta or rice and a salad. *Serves 4.*

FISH & SEAFOOD

"Añejo" (aged) Tequila

When most people think of tequila they automatically think of a potent clear liquid. Although most tequila is a silver or white color there are other varieties and colors of tequila on the market.

A small amount of tequila is aged from one to seven years and is classified "añejo" meaning aged. If it is stored in oak barrels that had been used to store bourbon, brandy or wine the tequila takes on a gold or amber color. When the manufacturer mixes an almond flavoring with the tequila it is then called "Crema de Tequila".

Although the flavor and quality of tequila may vary from maker to maker—what is considered the "best" tequila is a matter of individual taste.

VERACRUZ SHRIMP

I had my first lesson in Spain on how good shrimp, tomatoes and olives were together. Back in the Southwest I took this dish one step further, adding the chile. It creates a sublime taste. Serve it with plain rice or add a little saffron if your budget will allow.

3 Tbsp. OLIVE OIL divided in half
3 Tbsp. BUTTER divided in half
4 GREEN ONIONS, chopped (include greens)
6 ripe TOMATOES, peeled and chopped
2 Tbsp. fresh PARSLEY, finely chopped
1 tsp. CILANTRO, chopped
1 tsp. SALT
1/2 tsp. ground WHITE PEPPER
1/2 cup GREEN CHILE, chopped
1/2 cup TEQUILA
2 cloves GARLIC, run through a garlic press
36 large deveined SHRIMP
COOKED RICE
sprigs of CILANTRO
GREEN OLIVES, chopped

Heat the oil and butter in a large frying pan and sauté the green onions, chile, garlic and shrimp for 5 minutes. Add the rest of the ingredients, except the rice, sprigs of cilantro and green olives, and cook for 2 - 3 more minutes or until the shrimp turn pink and are done. Do not overcook as the shrimp will be tough and you'll lose the fresh, clean taste of the vegetables. Serve over rice, garnish with sprigs of cilantro and chopped green olives. *Serves 6.*

SHRIMP FIESTA

This is a popular dish in many restaurants in Mexico. I made as many trips as possible south of the border to sample it. My excuse was that I was trying to ascertain just what it contained!

6 slices of BACON, cut into 24 pieces
24 LARGE SHRIMP, with the shells removed, and deveined
2 Tbsp. OLIVE OIL
1 Tbsp. BUTTER
2 cloves GARLIC, split in half
2 - 3 JALAPEÑOS, chopped
1/4 cup TEQUILA

Blanch the bacon in water for 5 minutes. Drain and pat dry on paper towels. Wrap a piece of bacon around each shrimp and secure with a toothpick. Heat the oil and melt the butter in a large frying pan, stir in the garlic and jalapeños and add the bacon wrapped shrimp and sauté for 6 - 7 minutes or until the shrimp are cooked. Remove from pan and place on a warmed platter. Deglaze the pan with the tequila, pour over the shrimp and serve with rice. *Serves 4.*

MARGARITA SHRIMP

One of the great things about this dish is—it is so easy. Use frozen shrimp, serve with rice or angel hair pasta and a green salad to create a great meal for drop-in company.

2 Tbsp. OLIVE OIL
1 clove GARLIC, run through a garlic press
1 tsp. CILANTRO, chopped
24 large SHRIMP, shelled and deveined
1 tsp LIME JUICE
1 Tbsp. TEQUILA
1/2 Tbsp. TRIPLE SEC

Heat oil, stir in garlic, cilantro and shrimp and sauté for 5 minutes. Stir in lime juice, tequila and triple sec and continue cooking for 3 - 4 minutes or until the shrimp turn pink and are done Serve over rice or angel hair pasta. *Serves 4.*

SHRIMP JALISCO

1 lb. LARGE SHRIMP, deveined, shelled
1 cup TEQUILA, divided
1 Tbsp. fresh LIME JUICE
1 JALAPEÑO, chopped
1 tsp. GROUND BLACK PEPPER
1 cup ALL-PURPOSE FLOUR
2 EGGS
1 tsp. RED CHILE POWDER or PAPRIKA
OIL for frying

Place the shrimp in a large, shallow glass dish. Mix together 1/2 cup of the tequila, lime juice, jalapeño and black pepper and pour over the shrimp. Chill in the refrigerator for 2 hours.

Mix flour with the remaining 1/2 cup of tequila, eggs and red chile powder. Drain the shrimp and dip into the batter. Deep fry in hot oil for 5 minutes or until golden brown. Serve with **Sauce Jalisco**. *Serves 4.*

SAUCE JALISCO

1/4 cup SESAME OIL
1/4 cup LIGHT SOY SAUCE
1/4 cup TEQUILA
1 tsp. FRESH GINGER, grated
1 clove GARLIC, run through a garlic press.

Put all the ingredients together in a sauce pan, warm over low heat and serve.

TEQUILA BASTED HALIBUT

1/2 cup TEQUILA
1 Tbsp. OLIVE OIL
1 tsp. dried TARRAGON
1/2 tsp. LEMON PEEL, grated
1/2 tsp. freshly ground BLACK PEPPER
1 clove GARLIC, run through a garlic press
1 1/2 to 2 lbs. HALIBUT STEAKS, approximately 1 inch thick

Mix together the tequila, olive oil, tarragon, lemon peel, pepper and garlic. Place halibut steaks in a shallow glass dish and pour tequila mixture over them. Cover with plastic wrap and refrigerate for 6 - 8 hours, turning occasionally. Drain the fish, reserving the marinade. Grill the fish over hot coals or broil in the oven for approximately five minutes on each side or until the fish flakes when touched with the tines of a fork. Brush the marinade over the fish at least once during the cooking process then discard the marinade. *Serves 4.*

HALIBUT POACHED IN MILK & TEQUILA

Preheat oven to 375 degrees.

4 HALIBUT STEAKS
1 cup MILK
1/4 cup TEQUILA
1/2 pint WHIPPING CREAM
1/4 cup prepared HORSERADISH

Wash the halibut steaks and place in a large shallow baking dish. Mix the milk and tequila together and pour over the fish. Bake in a 375 degree oven for 30 minutes or until the fish flakes when touched with a fork.

While the fish is cooking, whip the cream and stir in the horseradish. When the fish is done, remove from the poaching liquid, place on individual plates, top with a dollop of the cream and horseradish mixture and serve at once. *Serves 4.*

FISH a la FREDERICKSBURG

1/4 cup BUTTER
1/2 cup SLIVERED ALMONDS
1 Tbsp. fresh PARSLEY or 1 tsp dried
1 Tbsp. fresh DILL WEED or 1 tsp. dried
4 WHITE FISH FILETS such as Sole or Flounder
1/4 cup TEQUILA
2 Tbsp. LEMON JUICE

Melt the butter in a frying pan, stir in almonds, parsley and dill. Add fish to the pan and sauté for 2 minutes on each side. Mix tequila and lemon juice together, pour over fish and simmer for 5 - 7 minutes or until fish flakes when touched with a fork. *Serves 4.*

THE LION'S LOBSTER

Born under the sign of Leo I like center stage and rich food. When asked "what would you like to eat for your birthday?" my reply is always "lobster." This past year my wife, Guylyn, tired of serving lobster with simple melted or drawn butter, came up with this. Now I can say "I want the lobster—just like we had it last year."

1 LEMON, cut in half
1/4 cup CHOPPED CELERY LEAVES
4 (6 to 8 oz.) LOBSTER TAILS (if frozen let thaw)
1/2 lb. BUTTER
1/4 cup TEQUILA
1 tsp. CHILE ARBOL, crushed

Put the lemon halves, and celery leaves in a large pot of water and bring to a boil. Plunge the lobster tails in the water and cook for 7 - 9 minutes or until done. While they are cooking, melt the butter in a saucepan, stir in the tequila and chile and keep warm.

When the lobster tails are done, drain, cut the shells with kitchen shears and arrange the lobster tails on a plate with parsleyed potatoes, wild rice or your favorite pasta. Pour the butter into four small bowls and serve to dip the lobster in. A crusty loaf of French bread will help you sop up any remaining butter. *Serves 4.*

MARINATED SWORDFISH STEAK

Preheat oven to 375 degrees.

1/2 cup LIGHT SOY SAUCE
1 1/2 cups TEQUILA
1 Tbsp. FRESH GINGER or 1 tsp. dried, ground
2 cloves GARLIC
4 SWORDFISH STEAKS, approximately 1/2 inch thick
2 cups MILK

Mix the soy sauce, 1 cup of the tequila, ginger and garlic together. Place fish steaks in a shallow glass bowl. Pour tequila mixture over fish, cover and marinate in the refrigerator for 2 hours. Remove from the refrigerator and let stand at room temperature for 1/2 hour and drain.

Mix together the milk, the remaining 1/2 cup of tequila and bake in a 375 degree oven for 30 minutes or until fish flakes easily with a fork. Drain off the liquid and serve with rice, lemon slices and **Cantaloupe Salsa** (see page 90). *Serves 4.*

Tequila and the Arts

Tequila has had a lasting influence on the arts—particularly the songs and dances of Mexico. One of my favorite dances is where two costumed dancers end their performance when the girl, dressed in a colorful skirt with layers of petticoats, dances in a tight circle around her partner's hat and a bottle of tequila. The dance is considered a success if both the hat and the bottle remain untrampled by the dancers' flying feet.

GRILLED YELLOWFIN TUNA

1 Tbsp. ORANGE JUICE
2 Tbsp. OLIVE OIL
4 (6 oz.) YELLOWFIN TUNA STEAKS, 3/4 to 1 inch thick

Mix together the orange juice and oil and brush over the tuna steaks. Grill the steaks either on an indoor cooker or over hot coals for 8 - 10 minutes or until fish flakes easily when touched with a fork. Garnish with twisted orange slices and serve with **Orange-Tequila Sauce**. *Serves 4.*

ORANGE-TEQUILA SAUCE

1 cup MAYONNAISE
1/4 cup TEQUILA
1 tsp. grated ORANGE PEEL
1/4 cup ORANGE JUICE
1 tsp. RED CHILE FLAKES such as PEQUIN

Mix together mayonnaise, tequila, orange peel, orange juice and red chile flakes. Cover the sauce with plastic wrap and chill in refrigerator for one hour.

MEAT DISHES

The Legends of Pulque

Pulque was the stuff that legends were made of. One tale is about a nobleman named Papantzin, in the reign of Tecpancaltzin (990-1042 A.D.), who discovered the secret of obtaining the juice from the maguey plant. Since he and his friends found it so delightful, Papantzin decided to use the drink to persuade the King to marry his daughter, Princess Xochitl. The plan must have worked since Tecpancaltzin sired a son by the Princess.

When tequila evolved from pulque and became the more popular drink, writers took up their pens and started to immortalize it. Today, modern day song-writers pen such songs about tequila as Cindy Jordan's popular *Jose Cuervo* and Herb Alpert's *Tequila*.

SOUTHWESTERN BEEF STEW

Usually—beef stew is beef stew is beef stew is—well you get the message. That is until you add a little red chile and tequila, then it is a great southwestern beef stew!

1 1/2 lb. **BONELESS ROUND STEAK,**
    cut into bite-size pieces
1/4 cup **ALL-PURPOSE FLOUR**
1 tsp. **RED CHILE POWDER**
4 Tbsp. **OLIVE OIL**
1 **ONION,** chopped
1 can (14 1/2 oz.) **BEEF BROTH**
1 Tbsp. **WORCESTERSHIRE SAUCE**
1/4 cup **TEQUILA**
4 cups **WATER**
1 can (28 oz.) chopped **TOMATOES**
2 cloves **GARLIC,** cut in half
1 **JALAPEÑO,** chopped
4 medium **CARROTS,** sliced
4 medium **TURNIPS,** peeled, quartered
6 medium **POTATOES,** peeled, quartered

    Put flour and red chile powder in a plastic bag, add the beef chunks and shake until coated. Heat oil in a large, heavy Dutch oven or pot, stir in onion, then the beef and brown on all sides. Add beef broth, Worcestershire sauce, tequila, water, tomatoes, garlic and jalapeño. Cook over medium heat for 1 hour. Add carrots, turnips, and potatoes and cook for another hour or until the vegetables are tender. Serve with generous helpings of French bread. *Serves 6.*

JALAPA HAMBURGERS

Jalapeños are named after Jalapa, the capital of Veracruz, Mexico. The jalapeños coupled with the tequila give these hamburgers a great lift.

2 lbs. GROUND BEEF
1 tsp. WORCESTERSHIRE SAUCE
1/4 cup TORTILLA CHIPS, finely crushed
1 tsp. DIJON MUSTARD
1 JALAPEÑO, chopped
1/2 tsp. ground BLACK PEPPER
1/4 cup TEQUILA

Mix all ingredients together and form into equal sized patties. Grill over charcoal, fry or broil until done to taste.   Serve on Mexican rolls or in pita bread.   *Serves 4 - 6.*

BEEF, PEPPER & ONION KABOBS

1 lb. BONELESS BEEF SIRLOIN, cut into 1 inch cubes
2 WHITE ONIONS, cut into eighths
1 RED BELL PEPPER, cut into wedges
1 GREEN BELL PEPPER, cut into wedges
1 tsp. SESAME OIL
2 tsp. LIGHT SOY SAUCE
1/4 cup TEQUILA
1 cup WATER
2 cloves GARLIC, cut in half

Thread the beef, onions, and bell pepper on skewers and place in a large plate or pan. Mix together oil, soy sauce, tequila, garlic and water and pour over kabobs. Cover and marinate in the refrigerator for 2 hours turning at least twice.

Remove from the refrigerator and let stand until room temperature (about 1/2 hour).   Grill over hot coals for 6 - 7 minutes or until beef is done to taste. Serve with rice or polenta and a green salad. *Serves 4.*

GRILLED MUSTARD STEAKS

4 (6 - 8 oz.) SIRLOIN or RIB EYE STEAKS, approx. 1/2" thick
1 tsp. coarse ground BLACK PEPPER
2 Tbsp. HONEY MUSTARD
1/2 tsp. WORCESTERSHIRE SAUCE
1 cup TEQUILA
1 tsp. PEQUIN CHILE FLAKES

Place the steaks in a shallow dish. Mix pepper, mustard, Worcestershire, tequila and chile together and pour over steaks. Marinate in the refrigerator for 3 - 4 hours, remove and let stand at room temperature for 1/2 hour. Remove the steaks from marinade and grill over hot coals to taste, basting twice with the marinade. Discard the remainder of the marinade. Serve the steaks with potato salad and whole onions roasted over the barbecue. *Serves 4.*

MEXICAN STYLE POT ROAST

1 Tbsp. RED CHILE POWDER
1/4 cup ALL-PURPOSE FLOUR
1 3 1/2 lb. SIRLOIN TIP or ROUND ROAST
1/2 cup plus 1 Tbsp. TEQUILA
2 Tbsp. OLIVE OIL
1 ONION, chopped
1 can (28 oz.) CRUSHED TOMATOES
1/2 cup GREEN CHILE, chopped
1 Tbsp. CILANTRO, chopped
1 tsp. ground BLACK PEPPER

Mix red chile and flour together. Wet the roast with 1 Tbsp. tequila and pat the chile flour mixture onto the roast. Heat oil in a heavy Dutch oven or pot and sear the roast on all sides over high heat. Turn down heat, add the rest of the tequila, onions, tomatoes, green chile, cilantro, and pepper. Cover and cook over low heat for 2 hours or until the pot roast is tender.

Serve with potato pancakes and a green salad. *Serves 4 - 6.*

LAKE CHAPALA STIR FRY

Mexico's Lake Chapala is a popular nesting ground for "snow birds" from the United States. One friend of ours spends every winter there and this is one of the meals she serves to guests on her secluded patio near the lake.

1 lb. BEEF FLANK STEAK
1 cup TEQUILA
1 tsp. CRUSHED RED PEQUIN CHILE
2 Tbsp. OLIVE OIL
1 Tbsp. SESAME OIL
2 cloves GARLIC, run through a garlic press
1/2 Tbsp. fresh GINGER, grated
4 GREEN ONIONS, chopped
1 RED BELL PEPPER, cut into strips
1 cup SNOW PEAS
1 pkg. (8 oz.) frozen BABY CORN, thawed
2 Tbsp. LIGHT SOY SAUCE

Cut beef flank steak lengthwise into 2 pieces. Cut each strip across the grain into 1/4" strips. Place beef in a shallow glass bowl. Combine tequila with red chile flakes and pour over beef. Marinate in refrigerator for 1 hour. Drain, and discard marinade.

Heat 1 tablespoon of the olive oil in a wok or large, non-stick frying pan. Cook beef for 2 - 3 minutes, stirring constantly. Remove from pan.

Add the rest of the olive oil and sesame oil to the wok and stir in garlic, ginger, bell pepper, pea pods and stir fry for approximately 30 seconds. Add corn and green onions and cook another 30 seconds, stirring constantly. Return meat to the pan. Add the soy sauce and heat through. Serve at once over rice. Great served with tropical fruit salad. *Serves 4 - 6.*

THE STEW'S THE THING

This is a wonderful stew that requires very slow cooking. And, no, —you're not reading it wrong—it takes an equal amount of onions and beef and a half a cup of paprika. Trust me, it's wonderful with noodles and black bread on a cold winter's night.

4 Tbsp. OLIVE OIL
2 lbs. YELLOW ONIONS
2 lbs. LEAN STEWING BEEF, cut into bite size pieces
1/2 cup PAPRIKA
1 cup TEQUILA
1 can (6 oz.) TOMATO PASTE

Heat olive oil in a heavy pan or Dutch oven and sauté the onions until limp. Add beef, and paprika and brown the meat. Add the rest of the ingredients and cook over very low heat* for 3 - 4 hours or until the meat is tender. *Serves 4 - 6.*

*I use a heat shield over the burner to prevent the stew from sticking.

CORNED BEEF
SOUTHWESTERN STYLE

The addition of tequila and celery leaves gives corned beef a great new taste.

2 1/2 to 3 lb. CORNED BEEF BRISKET
1/2 cup TEQUILA
1 cup WATER
1 cup CELERY TOPS AND LEAVES
1 Tbsp. fresh PARSLEY, chopped
1 JALAPEÑO, diced

Rinse corned beef under running water and place in a crock pot or slow cooker. Add the rest of the ingredients and cook on low for 8 hours or until the corned beef is tender. Serve with new potatoes and steamed cabbage. *Serves 4 - 6.*

MAC'S SPECIAL MEATLOAF

We get tired of meatloaf and go for weeks eating all those "good for you" chicken and fish dishes—lightly sauced and garnished with slivered vegetables. Then we just have to have some good old meatloaf—except this is just like the title says—special.

Preheat oven to 350 degrees.

1 lb. LEAN GROUND BEEF
1/2 lb. LEAN GROUND PORK
1/2 cup TEQUILA
1 Tbsp. WORCESTERSHIRE SAUCE
1 cup SEASONED BREAD CRUMBS
1/2 tsp. ground BLACK PEPPER
2 EGGS, lightly beaten
3 - 4 GREEN ONIONS, chopped (white portion only)
2 cloves GARLIC, run through a garlic press
1 tsp. SALT
1 Tbsp. fresh PARSLEY, chopped
1/2 cup TEQUILA SALSA*
1/2 cup PROVOLONE CHEESE, cubed

Mix all ingredients together except cheese and spray a loaf pan with spray release. Put 1/2 of meat mixture into pan. Lay cheese cubes on top of meat. Cover cheese with the rest of the meat. Bake in a 350 degree oven for 45 minutes or until the meat is cooked through. *Serve with **Tequila Salsa** (see page 89) on the side. *Serves 4 - 6.*

Tequila is Back in Style!

Tequila, like many other products, goes through stages of popularity. Fashionable during the late fifties and early sixties, it suffered an image problem in the seventies.

With the advent of the southwestern craze in the eighties and nineties tequila again became in vogue. Along with other clear beverages such as gin, vodka and rum, tequila is now reportedly gaining in popularity over the darker whiskeys such as bourbon and Scotch.

HIDALGO STEW

2 lbs. LEAN STEWING BEEF
1 can (14 1/2 oz.) BEEF BOUILLON
1 cup TEQUILA
2 ONIONS, coarsely chopped
2 Tbsp. RED CHILE POWDER
1 lb. fresh MUSHROOMS, chopped
3 cups WATER
2 CARROTS, diced
1 TURNIP, diced
1 can (28 oz.) WHOLE PEELED TOMATOES, diced
1 1/2 cups SMALL GREEN PEAS

Place all ingredients, except peas, in a crockpot or slow cooker and cook on low 7 hours. Add peas and cook for an hour longer or until meat is tender. Serve with rice or noodles. *Serves 6 - 8.*

CARNE A LA CARLOS

1/2 lb. BUTTER or MARGARINE
2 cloves GARLIC, run through a garlic press
1 Tbsp. DRIED RED CHILE FLAKES such as PEQUIN
1 Tbsp. CILANTRO, chopped
1/4 cup GREEN CHILE, chopped
2 Tbsp. TEQUILA
4 (8 oz.) NEW YORK STRIP STEAKS

Blend the butter, garlic, red chile, cilantro, green chile and tequila in a processor and refrigerate for an hour before serving. Broil the steaks to desired doneness, put 1/4 of the butter/chile mixture on top of each steak and serve at once. *Serves 4.*

BARBECUE BEEF BRISKET

Like most people I don't have a large brick oven to roast my brisket in so I make my barbecue brisket in a long, rather laborious two step operation. However, it always seems worthwhile as we have served it many times to our catering customers and get great comments.

Preheat oven to 275 degrees.

8 - 10 lbs. BEEF BRISKET,
   trimmed and washed
2 cups TEQUILA

4 cups WATER
1 pkg. prepared ONION
   SOUP MIX

Place brisket in a large roasting pan. Mix together tequila, water, and onion soup mix. Pour over brisket, cover with aluminum foil and bake in a 275 degree oven for 8 - 10 hours or until the brisket is tender.

Let brisket cool to room temperature, take it out of the pan, wrap it in foil and refrigerate for at least 6 hours. Slice across the grain while still cold, layer in a large pan, cover with **Our Best Barbecue Sauce** and heat in a 350 degree oven for 30 - 45 minutes or until warmed through. Serve at once with potato salad, cole slaw, rolls and one of the tequila goodies from the dessert section of this book. *Serves 12 - 18.*

OUR BEST BARBECUE SAUCE

2 cups CATSUP
1/4 cup MAPLE SYRUP
1/4 cup ORANGE
   MARMALADE
1/4 cup PREPARED
   MUSTARD
2 cloves GARLIC, run
   through a garlic press

1/2 ONION, finely chopped
2 tsp. WORCESTERSHIRE
   SAUCE
1/2 tsp. SALT
1 tsp. ground BLACK PEPPER
2 JALAPEÑOS, diced
1/4 cup LEMON JUICE
1/2 cup TEQUILA

Put all the ingredients in a saucepan and cook over medium heat until it comes to a boil, remove from heat and pour over the sliced brisket before reheating the meat.

SUNDAY DINNER FOR TWO

Cooking for two is not always easy. Try this simple beef dinner for Sunday or any happy occasion.

1 ROUND STEAK (3/4 - 1 lb.), cut into four pieces
1/2 cup all-purpose FLOUR
1 Tbsp. RED CHILE POWDER
1 tsp. coarse ground BLACK PEPPER
3 - 4 Tbsp. OLIVE OIL
1 cup TEQUILA
2 cups WATER
2 cloves GARLIC, run through a garlic press
1/2 cup CELERY LEAVES
2 cups ripe TOMATOES, peeled and chopped

Mix flour, chile powder, and pepper together and dredge the meat in the flour mixture. Heat oil in a large heavy pot such as a Dutch oven and brown meat on all sides. Mix water, tequila, garlic, celery leaves and tomatoes, pour over meat and cook, over low heat, for 1 & 1/2 to 2 hours or until meat is tender.

Serve with parsleyed new potatoes or mashed potatoes and turnips. *Serves 2.*

GINGER GLAZED PORK CHOPS

Preheat oven to 375 degrees.

2 Tbsp. OLIVE OIL
6 - 8 BUTTERFLIED, CENTER-CUT PORK CHOPS
1 tsp. LIGHT SOY SAUCE
1/3 cup ORANGE JUICE
1/2 cup TEQUILA
1 Tbsp. fresh GINGER, grated
1/2 cup WATER
ORANGE SLICES

Heat oil in a large frying pan, and brown chops on both sides. Place chops in baking dish. Mix together soy sauce, orange juice, tequila, ginger and water and pour over chops. Cover with aluminum foil, and bake in a 375 degree oven for 45 minutes. Uncover and bake for 15 more minutes or until chops are done. Add more orange juice, tequila and water if the juice evaporates too rapidly. Serve garnished with thin slices of orange. *Serves 4.*

MY FAVORITE PORK ROAST

The combination of fruit and tequila gives this pork roast a subtle, superb flavor. I prefer Granny Smith apples in this recipe.

Preheat oven to 375 degrees.

3 1/2 to 4 lb. PORK ROAST
1 tsp. dried ROSEMARY, crushed
1 Tbsp. coarsely ground BLACK PEPPER
2 cloves GARLIC, peeled and cut into quarters
2 APPLES, cored and sliced
1/2 cup DRIED PRUNES
1 cup TEQUILA
1/2 cup ORANGE JUICE
1 cup WATER

Rub the pepper and rosemary into the roast. With a sharp knife make slits in the roast and stick the garlic into them.

Place the pork in a roasting pan. Surround the roast with the apples and prunes. Mix together tequila, orange juice and water and pour around (not over) the roast. Bake for 30 minutes at 375 degrees. Reduce the heat to 325 degrees, baste the roast with the pan juice and continue baking for 1 1/2 - 2 hours or until the roast is done. Strain juice and discard fruit. Serve sliced pork with pan juices. *Serves 4 - 6.*

GLAZED HOLIDAY HAM

Preheat oven to 325 degrees.

1/2 HAM BUTT (5 - 6 pounds)
1 cup ORANGE MARMALADE
1/2 cup TEQUILA
1/4 cup ORANGE FLAVORED LIQUEUR
2 tsp. DIJON OR BEER MUSTARD
1 tsp. ground CLOVES
1/2 tsp. ground GINGER

Rinse ham under cold running water and place in a baking pan. Mix together the rest of the ingredients and pour over the ham. Bake in a 325 degree oven for 3 1/2 to 4 hours, basting occasionally. Let cool for 15 to 20 minutes before slicing and serving. Great served with **Aunt Reuy's Special Sauce**!. *Serves 8 - 10.*

AUNT REUY'S SPECIAL SAUCE

This is my adaptation of a favorite family recipe.

1 cup CURRANT JELLY
1/2 cup DIJON MUSTARD
1/2 cup MAYONNAISE
1/4 cup TEQUILA

Mix all the ingredients together and refrigerate until ready to serve. A spoonful of this is great with ham, cold roast beef or cold sliced chicken.

PORK MEDALLIONS WITH TEQUILA-PEACH SAUCE

4 Tbsp. OLIVE OIL
1 Tbsp. RED CHILE POWDER
1 tsp. ground BLACK PEPPER
1/2 tsp. CUMIN
1 tsp. dried PARSLEY FLAKES
8 PORK MEDALLIONS*
1/2 cup TEQUILA
1/2 cup PEACHES (fresh or canned)
1/4 tsp. ground CINNAMON
pinch of ground GINGER
2 Tbsp. LIME JUICE
2 - 3 GREEN ONIONS, chopped (include greens)

Heat oil in a frying pan. Stir chile powder, pepper, cumin and parsley into oil. Sauté pork medallions for 8 - 10 minutes, turning two or three times until the pork is done. Remove to a warm platter and keep warm.

Blend 1/4 cup of the tequila, peaches, cinnamon, ginger and lime juice. Pour remaining 1/4 cup of tequila in the hot frying pan and stir to deglaze the pan. Add tequila-peach mixture and cook over high heat for 3 - 4 minutes, stirring constantly until slightly reduced. Pour over the warm pork medallions and serve garnished with chopped green onions. *Serves 4.*

*If your supermarket doesn't carry the medallions—buy thin pork chops and cut the center off the bone to make your own.

VEGETABLE DISHES

Is it Aguardiente de Agave, Mescal, or Tequila?

Although it's impossible to pin-point the exact date, the name of the town *Tequila* became synonymous with the name of the liquor sometime around the turn of the century.

An award was presented at the Chicago World's Fair of 1893 to "Mescal Brandy" made in the town of Tequila. In 1910 "Tequila Wine" was given an award in San Antonio, Texas.

From then on most books and records indicate that tequila became the accepted word, although labels of tequila often have some reference to "aguardiente de agave" or "mescal" even to this day.

EGGPLANT CULIACAN STYLE

Preheat oven to 350 degrees.

1 large EGGPLANT
2 Tbsp. coarse (Kosher) SALT
WATER
3 Tbsp. OLIVE OIL
1 medium ONION
1 lb. lean GROUND BEEF or GROUND TURKEY
1 Tbsp. RED CHILE
1 tsp. dried OREGANO
1/2 tsp. dried BASIL
1 clove GARLIC, minced
1 Tbsp. fresh PARSLEY (or 1 tsp. dried)
1/4 tsp. ground NUTMEG
1 cup TEQUILA
1 can (28 oz.) PEELED TOMATOES, with the juice
1 cup MOZZARELLA CHEESE, shredded
1/4 cup FRESHLY GRATED ROMANO CHEESE

Peel the eggplant and cut into 1 inch slices. Soak in water with 2 tablespoons salt for 1/2 hour. Drain under cold running water and dry on paper towels. Heat oil in a large frying pan and sauté the onions and ground meat. Stir in chile, oregano, basil, garlic, parsley, nutmeg, tequila and tomatoes and cook over medium heat for 30 minutes.

Layer eggplant in a large greased baking dish, spoon the tomato mixture over eggplant, top with the mozzarella, then the Romano and bake in a 350 degree oven for 30 minutes or until heated through and cheese is lightly browned. *Serves 4 - 6.*

Mescal and Tequila

The Spaniards probably ran out of their supply of hard liquor soon after landing in the New World. Before building their stills, they had to find raw ingredients that would distill into a liquor they could enjoy.

If they had turned their attention to corn, bourbon might be exported from Mexico instead of made in Kentucky. And, although they introduced grape vines and sugar cane into Mexico, the Spanish King discouraged commercial cultivation of these crops because it was in open conflict with the economic interests of Spain itself.

They found that pulque, the fermented drink made by the Indians was not strong enough and was too sweet for their taste. They soon discovered that other species of the plant would produce a stronger drink after distillation—and hence, mescal (spelled mezcal in Mexico) and subsequently tequila were created.

The Indians frowned on drinking anything stronger than pulque. However, they soon took to these new spirits which caused problems. Greedy mine operators would get the natives drunk on mescal and kidnap them from their work on farms to make them laborers in the mines. Drunkenness also provoked crimes and public disorder.

These problems prompted the colonial government which had at first allowed the production of mescal to later stop manufacture altogether.

All this changed in the nineteenth century. The Mexican government, although it made strict rules and regulations about the manufacture of mescal and tequila, realized that tequila was an extremely valuable export and a good source of income.

CHEESE FONDUE

The first time I had a cheese fondue was while witnessing a bizarre, surrealistic performance of an unpublished play. The acting was abysmal but the fondue was delicious and so, over the years, I've experimented with different forms of this pleasurable dish. I think this one is sublime and deserves applause.

1 clove GARLIC, peeled and split in half
1 lb. SWISS CHEESE, grated
1 & 1/2 cups TEQUILA
1/4 tsp. SALT (optional)
1/2 tsp. ground WHITE PEPPER
2 Tbsp. CORNSTARCH
3 Tbsp. WATER

Rub the garlic on the sides and bottom of a deep baking dish with a glazed interior (do not use metal). Put the cheese, tequila, salt, and pepper in the pan and cook, over medium heat, stirring constantly, until all the cheese has melted. Stir cornstarch into water until you make a smooth paste. Whisk into cheese mixture and cook over medium heat for 2 to 3 minutes, stirring constantly until the mixture is nice and creamy. Set the pan over a chafing dish flame or candle warmer to serve.

Put your favorite vegetables, chunks of bread, warm meat balls, chunks of cooked ham or apples on fondue forks and dip into the cheese. *Serves 4 - 6.*

GREEN CHILE QUICHE

Quiche was one of the featured dishes on the menu of our restaurant when all the furor over the book that pondered the question whether real men ate quiche hit the media. After a hurried consultation with all involved, I decided to add green chile to our quiche and we continued to sell it to real men and everybody else.

Preheat oven to 375 degrees.

2 ONIONS, peeled, chopped
3 Tbsp. OLIVE OIL
1 1/2 Tbsp. all-purpose FLOUR
2 EGGS, lightly beaten
2/3 cup MILK
1/4 cup TEQUILA
1 tsp. SALT
1/2 tsp. ground WHITE PEPPER
1/4 tsp. ground CUMIN
1/4 tsp. ground OREGANO
1/2 cup grated CHEDDAR CHEESE
1/2 cup GREEN CHILE, chopped
1 (9 inch) PASTRY SHELL
1/4 cup SWISS CHEESE, shredded

Sauté onions in olive oil until limp. Sprinkle flour over onions and cook for 2 - 3 minutes, stirring constantly. Let cool. Beat tequila, salt, pepper, cumin and oregano into the eggs. Stir in Cheddar cheese and chile. Pour the mixture into an unbaked 9 inch pastry shell. Sprinkle Swiss cheese over the top and bake in a 375 degree oven for 30 minutes or until the center is set and the top is lightly browned. *Serves 6.*

ZUCCHINI TOSS

2 Tbsp. BUTTER
3 Tbsp. OLIVE OIL
3 medium ZUCCHINI, washed, with the stems and
    bottoms cut off, and sliced into 1/4 inch rounds
1 tsp. RED CHILE
1 clove GARLIC, run through a garlic press
pinch of NUTMEG
1 tsp. FRESH ROSEMARY
1/4 cup TEQUILA
1 cup grated SWISS CHEESE

Melt butter in a frying pan, add oil and let heat. Add zucchini, chile, garlic, nutmeg and rosemary. Cook over medium heat, tossing the zucchini occasionally until tender. Stir in tequila, then turn into an ovenproof serving dish. Top with cheese and place under broiler for 2 - 3 minutes or until cheese has melted. Serve at once. *Serves 4 - 6.*

CORN FRITTERS

1 EGG, well beaten
1/4 cup MILK
2 Tbsp. TEQUILA
1 cup BISQUICK®
1 1/2 cups of WHOLE KERNEL CORN
1/4 cup diced PIMENTOS
OIL for deep frying
chopped GREEN ONIONS

Beat egg, milk, tequila, and Bisquick together. Stir in corn and pimentos and drop the batter by tablespoon into hot oil and fry until golden brown. Dry on paper towels, sprinkle with chopped green onions and serve. *Serves 4.*

TOMATO KRAUT

This makes a great side dish with roast pork or pork chops, or serve on top of your hot dogs.

1 lb. SAUERKRAUT
3 Tbsp. OLIVE OIL
1 ONION, peeled, chopped
2 tsp. PAPRIKA

1 can (6 oz.) TOMATO PASTE
1 tsp. CARAWAY SEED
1/2 cup TEQUILA
1/2 cup WATER

Place sauerkraut in a colander in the sink and squeeze the water out of the sauerkraut. Put oil in a heavy pan and sauté onion for 5 minutes, then add sauerkraut, paprika, tomato paste and caraway seed and cook for another 5 minutes.   Add tequila and water and simmer over low heat for 30 minutes. To serve, use a slotted spoon or tongs and let any liquid left drain off. Great served with grilled smoked sausages, sliced pork roast or prime rib. *Serves 4 - 6.*

NUTTY ONIONS

Whenever I do an onion dish I'm reminded of Ernest Hemingway's jab at Gertrude Stein when he responded to her "A rose is a rose is a rose . . ." with "An onion is an onion is an onion . . ."

Preheat oven to 350 degrees.

4 large ONIONS, peeled,
     cut in half across
     the middle
1 can (14 1/2 oz.) CHICKEN
     BROTH
1/2 cup TEQUILA
1 Tbsp. LEMON JUICE

1 tsp. CAYENNE PEPPER
1 clove GARLIC, run
     through garlic press
3 tsp. HONEY
1 Tbsp. BUTTER
1/2 cup PECANS, chopped

Place the onions in a baking pan. Put chicken broth, tequila, lemon juice, cayenne, garlic, honey and butter in a saucepan and cook over low heat until all the ingredients are blended through. Pour the liquid over onions and bake for 30 minutes. Take the pan out of the oven, sprinkle the pecans over onions, return to the oven and bake for 5 - 7 more minutes or until the nuts are lightly browned. *Serves 4.*

GLAZED CARROTS

6 medium CARROTS, washed and sliced
2 Tbsp. BUTTER
2 Tbsp. HONEY
1/4 cup TEQUILA
3 Tbsp. TRIPLE SEC
1/4 tsp. SALT
1/4 tsp. ground BLACK PEPPER

Place carrots in a saucepan with water to cover and cook over medium heat for approximately 30 minutes or until carrots are tender. Drain and return to the pan. Add the rest of the ingredients in the saucepan, stir well. Cook over low heat for 5 - 10 minutes until the carrots are nicely coated. *Serves 4 - 6.*

ACORN SQUASH
THE EASY WAY

Cooking acorn squash has been a long, laborious procedure until the advent of the microwave. Not only is this method fast but the squash has a nice texture when cooked.

2 medium ACORN SQUASH, cut in half lengthwise.
WATER
4 tsp. BUTTER
1 tsp. NUTMEG
pinch SALT
4 Tbsp. TEQUILA

Scrape seeds out of squash, and fill cavity half way with water. Cover each half with plastic wrap, place in the microwave and microwave on HIGH for 15 - 20 minutes or until squash is tender. Drain off any remaining water, let cool enough to handle, scrape out the meat of the squash and beat in the butter, nutmeg, salt and tequila. Place in a microwave safe bowl, cover with plastic wrap and microwave on HIGH for 5 minutes. *Serves 4.*

BRAISED CELERY

I discovered this recipe in 1974 when we opened our provincial French style restaurant. Every time I tried to take it off the menu and try something new my customers would demand its return.

1/2 cup BUTTER
1 stalk CELERY, washed - the ribs cut into
    slices about 1/2" thick
1/2 cup TEQUILA
1/4 cup WATER
1 tsp. SALT
1 tsp. ground WHITE PEPPER
2 Tbsp. ALL-PURPOSE FLOUR
1 cup WHIPPING CREAM
1/2 cup CHICKEN BROTH
1 cup SLIVERED ALMONDS

Melt butter in the top of double boiler, stir in celery, then add tequila, water, salt, pepper and cook over medium heat, stirring occasionally, until celery is tender. Sprinkle flour over the celery and stir. Then stir in cream and chicken stock and continue to cook in double boiler until the sauce thickens. Add almonds and the remaining 1/4 cup of tequila and cook for another 5 minutes. Serve as a side dish with prime rib, fish, or broiled chicken. *Serves 4.*

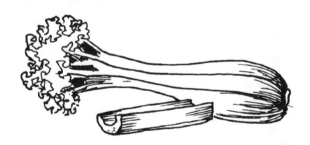

BAKED VEGETABLES MAZATLAN

Preheat oven to 350 degrees.

4 cups **SPINACH LEAVES, well washed and drained**
2 **YELLOW CROOKNECK SQUASH, diced**
2 **ZUCCHINI, diced**
2 **GREEN BELL PEPPERS, diced**
1 **ONION, chopped**
2 Tbsp. **RAISINS**
1/4 tsp. **ALLSPICE**
1 tsp. ground **CUMIN**
1 tsp. **RED CHILE POWDER**
    or 1/4 tsp. **CAYENNE**
1 cup **TOMATO JUICE**
1/4 cup **TEQUILA**
1/4 cup **SEASONED BREAD CRUMBS**
1/2 cup grated **PARMESAN CHEESE**
1/2 tsp. **PAPRIKA**
2 Tbsp. **BUTTER**

Layer half the spinach leaves in the bottom of a lightly greased baking dish. Mix together squash, zucchini, bell peppers, onions, raisins, allspice, cumin and chile and spread over the spinach leaves.

Mix together tomato juice and tequila and pour half of it over the vegetables. Layer rest of the spinach leaves on top of vegetables, pour the remaining tomato, tequila mixture over the top. Mix together bread crumbs, Parmesan cheese and chile powder and sprinkle over the top of the tomato mixture. Dot with butter and bake in a 350 degree oven for 45 minutes or until the casserole is hot and bubbly. *Serves 4 - 6.*

BRAISED ENDIVE

I do a lot of shows demonstrating food and/or selling and autographing my cookbooks. People often ask me how I come up with the recipes that are in the books. This is one example. Almost thirty years ago I was a guest at dinner in a swank Belgravia apartment in London and was served a braised endive dish. I asked my hostess for the recipe which she gave me. When I returned to the states I stashed it away and several years later when I retrieved it I decided to do some experimenting and changed the original dry sherry the cook had called for to tequila which I like better. Here is a much changed version of that original dish.

Preheat oven to 400 degrees.

4 Tbsp. BUTTER
4 BELGIAN ENDIVES
1/2 cup WHIPPING CREAM
1/4 cup TEQUILA
1/4 tsp. ground NUTMEG
1/4 tsp. SALT
1/4 tsp. ground WHITE PEPPER

Melt butter in a heavy pan and sauté endives on all sides, turning them very carefully with two forks. Then place in a shallow baking dish. Mix cream, tequila, nutmeg, salt and pepper together and pour over endives. Bake in a 400 degree oven for 10 minutes or until the endives are slightly brown and tender.

Serve on the side with such dishes as Veal Picatta or serve as an appetizer with crusty Italian or French bread. *Serves 4.*

ASPARAGUS IN ORANGE SAUCE

1 bunch (approx. 1 lb.) ASPARAGUS, washed and trimmed
1 tsp. grated ORANGE PEEL
1/2 cup ORANGE JUICE
1/4 cup TEQUILA
1/4 tsp. SALT
1/4 tsp. ground WHITE PEPPER
1 Tbsp. BUTTER

Place asparagus spears in a large frying pan. Stir together the rest of the ingredients, except butter, pour over asparagus and cook over medium heat for 8 - 10 minutes or until asparagus is tender. Remove asparagus from pan, place on a hot platter and hold. Stir butter in sauce and cook until the sauce is slightly reduced and smooth. Pour over the asparagus and serve. *Serves 4.*

SOUTH OF THE BORDER POTATOES

2 Tbsp. OLIVE OIL
1 Tbsp. BUTTER
3 large POTATOES, boiled, peeled and diced
3 - 4 GREEN ONIONS, chopped (include greens)
1/4 cup GREEN CHILE, chopped
1/2 Tbsp. RED BELL PEPPER, diced
2 Tbsp. TEQUILA

Heat oil and melt butter in a heavy frying pan. Stir in potatoes and onions and sauté for 10 minutes or until potatoes are lightly browned. Stir in chile, bell pepper and tequila and continue to cook for another five minutes. Serve with bacon and eggs for breakfast or serve with sliced cold roast beef or pork for lunch or dinner. *Serves 4.*

FETTUCCINE
WITH
RED PEPPER-TEQUILA SAUCE

1 pkg. (12 oz.) SPINACH FETTUCCINE
3 large RED BELL PEPPERS, with skins removed *
1/4 cup TEQUILA
1 cup SOUR CREAM
1 Tbsp. fresh BASIL
1/2 tsp. SALT
1/2 tsp. ground BLACK PEPPER

Place peppers in a food processor with tequila and purée. Cook fettuccine according to package directions. While it is cooking, heat the pepper and tequila mixture in a saucepan, stir in sour cream, basil, salt and pepper and cook until warm through.

Drain pasta, put on a large platter, spoon the pepper sauce over it, garnish with fresh basil leaves and serve. *Serves 4.*

*Cut the peppers in half, remove the seeds and membranes and place with the cut side down on a cookie sheet. Bake in a 400 degree oven for 30 minutes or until the skins on the peppers have blistered and turned black. Let the peppers cool just enough to handle and remove the skins.

SPICY BLACK-EYED PEAS

2 Tbsp. OLIVE OIL
1 ONION, chopped
1 clove, GARLIC
1 Tbsp. fresh PARSLEY
2 cans (15 oz. each) BLACK-EYED PEAS
1 can (15 oz.) WHOLE TOMATOES, chopped
1/4 cup TEQUILA
2 JALAPEÑOS, chopped
1/2 tsp. ground BLACK PEPPER

Heat oil in a saucepan, sauté onions for 4 - 5 minutes, add garlic, parsley, peas, tomatoes, tequila, jalapeños and pepper and simmer over low heat for 30 minutes or until warmed through. *Serves 4 - 6.*

SANTA FE STYLE MUSHROOMS

3 Tbsp. OLIVE OIL
1 lb. MUSHROOMS, washed and sliced
1 Tbsp. fresh PARSLEY
1 tsp. DILL WEED
1/2 tsp. ground WHITE PEPPER
1/2 tsp. PEQUIN CHILE FLAKES
1/4 cup TEQUILA
1 cup LOW FAT SOUR CREAM

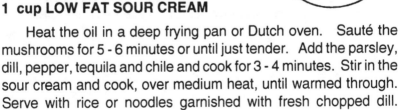

Heat the oil in a deep frying pan or Dutch oven. Sauté the mushrooms for 5 - 6 minutes or until just tender. Add the parsley, dill, pepper, tequila and chile and cook for 3 - 4 minutes. Stir in the sour cream and cook, over medium heat, until warmed through. Serve with rice or noodles garnished with fresh chopped dill. *Serves 4 - 6.*

TABASCO ONIONS

1/4 cup OLIVE OIL
1/8 lb. BUTTER
2 tsp. TABASCO® SAUCE
1 tsp. RED CHILE FLAKES
6 large YELLOW ONIONS, thinly sliced and cut in half
2 Tbsp. TEQUILA

Heat oil and melt butter in a large, heavy frying pan.   Stir in Tabasco sauce and red chile flakes.   Sauté onion slices until they start to soften, then add the tequila and continue to cook until soft, tossing occasionally with tongs or a large fork.   Serve with green enchiladas, steak or hamburgers. *Serves 4.*

PIMENTO SORBET

Sorbets have once again become popular. This makes a nice interlude between courses.

1 cup cooked red PIMENTOS
2 Tbsp. TEQUILA
1/4 cup LIME JUICE
1/4 cup WATER
1 Tbsp. SUGAR

Purée all the ingredients in a blender.   Pour into a saucepan and heat over medium high heat for 10 minutes, stirring occasionally.   Remove from heat and let mixture cool to room temperature. Pour into a metal freezing bowl and freeze, stirring two or three times during the freezing process or freeze in an ice cream or sorbet machine. *Serves 6 - 8.*

SALSAS & SAUCES

Who Invented the Margarita?

Many people have claimed to be the parent of the margarita. Several bartenders in the Los Angeles area say that they first thought of the concoction. One of these, Daniel Negrete, even says that he invented it when he managed a hotel in Puebla, Mexico and that there is an official document in Mexico City attesting to the fact.

Of course, in most of the stories the bartender blended the mixture of lime juice, orange flavored liqueur and tequila in honor of a girl—naturally very beautiful—naturally named Margarita.

Another story is that a lively, well liked hostess in San Antonio gave birth to the famous drink. The wife of a wealthy Texas rancher, she reportedly was addicted to tequila and put together the winning combination in her search for different ways to enjoy her favorite hooch.

The owner of a bar in Taxo, a bartender in Taos, a bartender in Mexico City and the entire staff of a race track in Tijuana also have laid claim to having the vision to invent the Margarita.

CRANBERRY & ORANGE SALSA

I was being interviewed about one of my books by a television host who acted horrified when, as she thumbed through the book on the air, she came across a recipe in which I had combined cranberries and chile. Being a rebel at heart, I decided to do some more testing and not only mix cranberries with chile but add my favorite liquor, tequila, as well. As shocking as it may seem on first glance this salsa makes a great addition to any holiday meal.

1/2 lb. CRANBERRIES
3 LARGE ORANGES
2 Tbsp. TEQUILA
1/4 cup GREEN CHILE, chopped
1/2 cup PECANS, chopped

Wash the cranberries and put in a food processor with the oranges and chop. Spoon into a bowl, add the tequila, green chile and pecans. Mix together, cover, and refrigerate until ready to use. Great to serve at holidays instead of the usual jellied cranberry sauce.

FRUIT SALSA

1 RED APPLE, cored, peeled and diced
1 GREEN APPLE (such as Granny Smith), cored, peeled and diced
2 Tbsp. LEMON JUICE
1/2 cup RAISINS
1/2 cup APRICOT PRESERVES
3 Tbsp. TEQUILA

Toss the apples with the lemon juice. Stir in the rest of the ingredients and chill in the refrigerator for half an hour before serving. Great served with sliced pork or ham.

AVOCADO SALSA

1 AVOCADO, finely chopped
2 tsp. LEMON JUICE
1 firm TOMATO, finely chopped
1 Tbsp. TEQUILA
1/2 ONION, chopped
1 clove GARLIC, run through a garlic press
1 tsp. RED CHILE FLAKES, such as pequin
1 tsp. CILANTRO, chopped
1/2 tsp. SALT

Pour the lemon juice over the avocado, then mix with the rest of the ingredients and serve with grilled fish, shrimp or chicken.

TEQUILA SALSA

1 cup GREEN CHILE, chopped
1/2 WHITE ONION, chopped
1 firm TOMATO, chopped
1/2 tsp. ground CUMIN
1/2 tsp. OREGANO, crushed
1 clove GARLIC, run through a garlic press
2 Tbsp. TEQUILA
1/2 tsp. SALT
1/2 tsp. ground BLACK PEPPER
1 tsp. CILANTRO, or parsley, chopped

Mix all the ingredients together and serve with tortilla chips or dishes such as **Mac's Special Meatloaf** (see page 65).

CANTALOUPE SALSA

This sweet/hot salsa is wonderful served with fish or roast pork.

**1 medium CANTALOUPE, peeled, seeded
    and finely chopped**
1 clove GARLIC, run through a garlic press
1 JALAPEÑO, seeded and chopped
1/2 tsp. SALT
1/2 tsp. ground WHITE PEPPER
2 Tbsp. LIME JUICE
2 Tbsp. TEQUILA
1 tsp. CILANTRO, chopped

    Mix all the ingredients together and refrigerate. Serve with dishes such as **Marinated Swordfish Steak** (see page 57).

CHINESE STYLE DIPPING SAUCE

1/4 cup LIGHT SOY SAUCE
2 Tbsp. SESAME OIL
1/4 cup TEQUILA
1/4 tsp. ground GINGER
3 GREEN ONIONS, chopped, (include greens)

    Mix all the ingredients together and serve to dip egg rolls, wonton, sushi, or pot stickers, or use over chop suey or chow mein instead of plain soy sauce.

SAUCE RANCHERO

This is a perfect sauce for your Huevos Rancheros or serve over scrambled eggs, or cooked vegetables such as cauliflower.

2 Tbsp. OLIVE OIL
1 ONION, chopped
2 cloves GARLIC, chopped
4 ribs CELERY, chopped
2 Tbsp. TEQUILA
2 cups ripe TOMATOES, chopped
1/2 cup GREEN CHILE, chopped
1 can (8 oz.) TOMATO SAUCE
1/2 tsp. ground CUMIN
1/2 tsp. SALT
1/2 tsp. ground BLACK PEPPER

Heat oil in a saucepan, stir in onion and garlic and celery and cook until soft.   Add the rest of the ingredients and cook, over low heat for 5 to 10 minutes.   Best served hot over eggs or vegetables.

DILLED MUSTARD SAUCE

2 Tbsp. PREPARED BROWN MUSTARD
1 CUCUMBER, seeded and diced
1/2 tsp. SALT
2 Tbsp. TEQUILA
1 tsp. dried DILL WEED
1/4 cup MAYONNAISE
1/4 cup SOUR CREAM

Mix all the ingredients together and chill in the refrigerator until ready to serve (will not keep more than a few hours).   Great with roast chicken or mix with mayonnaise and sour cream to dress potato salad.

It's better with butter! The following two "butters" are great enhancers for all sorts of vegetables and roast meats.

TEQUILA BUTTER

1/4 lb. BUTTER
1 tsp. NEW MEXICO RED CHILE POWDER
1 clove GARLIC run through a garlic press
1/2 Tbsp. TEQUILA
1 tsp. LIME JUICE

Mix all the ingredients together in a food processor. Use as a spread for "garlic" toast, or use on corn-on-the-cob or to heighten the taste of baked potatoes or fresh string beans. Or use in place of plain butter when making a grilled cheese sandwich.

JALAPEÑO BUTTER

1 JALAPEÑO
1 clove GARLIC
1/4 lb. BUTTER
1 Tbsp. TEQUILA

Chop the jalapeño and garlic in a food processor, using a steel blade. Add butter and tequila and process until smooth.

BREADS

Pulque and Pulquerias

Pulque is a fermented drink derived from the agave plant and is a great deal lower in alcoholic content than mescal or tequila and has long held a place in Mexican history. Historians believe the drink is approximately two thousand years old and played a prominent role in ancient Mexico—used by Indian priests to enhance their religious fervor, to commemorate victories, and celebrate good harvests. It was also thought to have great medicinal benefits and was said to have been given to sacrificial victims to ease their demise.

Pulque bars or pulquerias remained an integral part of Mexican life through the first part of this century. The pulqueria invariably had a sawdust or hard-packed dirt floor on which the customers spilled a little of the pulque so that Mother Earth could also quench her thirst. It was also a town or neighborhood meeting place where only pulque was served and the patrons could enjoy local gossip, card games and music along with their drinks.

APPLESAUCE BREAD

1 cup APPLESAUCE
2 EGGS, lightly beaten
1/4 lb. BUTTER
1/4 cup TEQUILA
2 cups all-purpose FLOUR
1/2 tsp. SALT

1/2 tsp. ground CINNAMON
1/2 tsp. ground ALLSPICE
1/2 cup BROWN SUGAR
3 tsp. BAKING POWDER
1/2 cup PECANS, chopped

Put eggs and butter in a food processor and blend until smooth and a lemon color.   Add the rest of the ingredients, except the pecans, and mix until batter is smooth.   Stir in pecans and then pour batter into 2 well-greased and lightly floured 9 x 5 x 3 inch loaf pans. Bake in a 350 degree oven for 45 minutes or until a toothpick inserted in the middle of the loaves comes out clean.   *Yield: 2 loaves.*

Rev 18 2002

BANANA NUT BREAD

Preheat oven to 350 degrees.

1 cup SUGAR
1/2 cup BUTTER or
    MARGARINE
2 EGGS, lightly beaten
3 RIPE BANANAS, mashed
2 cups all-purpose FLOUR

1/2 tsp. SALT
1 tsp. BAKING POWDER
1 tsp. BAKING SODA
1/4 cup TEQUILA
1/2 cup PECANS,
    chopped

Cream together sugar and butter, beat in the eggs, then bananas and then the flour.   Stir in salt, baking powder, soda, and tequila.   Stir in pecans and spoon into 2 lightly greased loaf pans and bake for 45 minutes or until a toothpick inserted in the center comes out clean. *Yield: 2 loaves.*

SOUTHWESTERN GARLIC BREAD

3 Tbsp. OLIVE OIL
3 Tbsp. MELTED BUTTER
4 cloves GARLIC, run through a garlic press
1 Tbsp. TEQUILA
2 tsp. LIME JUICE
1/2 tsp. RED CHILE POWDER
FRENCH BREAD

Mix together all the ingredients, except the bread, and brush on thick slices of French bread. Place under a broiler for 2 - 3 minutes until brown. Serve with black bean soup or spaghetti. *Serves 6 - 8.*

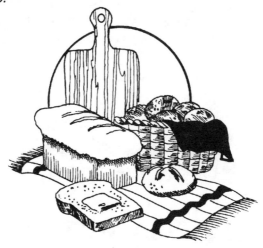

Tequila & Bonetti

Tequila shows up in the most unexpected places. One of my favorites was the dog named Tequila in the once popular TV show Tequila & Bonetti. *The gimmick was that the audience could hear the dog's every thought, couched in street jive such as "Get down with your bad self, home slice" while his master, Bonetti, an Italian cop from Brooklyn solved crimes in California.*

ESPECIAL FRENCH TOAST

The secret to making this is to use stale, French bread. If the bread is too fresh or soft it will tear after soaking in the egg mixture.

4 Tbsp. MILK
1 Tbsp. TEQUILA
1 tsp. GRAND MARNIER®
4 EGGS, well beaten
pinch of SALT
pinch of NUTMEG

pinch of CINNAMON
4 large or 8 small slices
   of stale FRENCH BREAD
2 Tbsp. BUTTER
LEMON JUICE
POWDERED SUGAR

Beat milk, tequila and Grand Marnier into the eggs, stir in salt, nutmeg and cinnamon. Place the bread in the egg mixture and let it absorb, turning two or three times.

Melt butter in a large frying pan and sauté the bread on both sides until lightly brown. Squeeze lemon juice over the hot toast and sprinkle a generous amount of powdered sugar on top. *Serves 4.*

TEQUILA MUFFINS

Preheat oven to 400 degrees.

2 cups all-purpose FLOUR
1/2 tsp. SALT
2 tsp. BAKING POWDER
2 Tbsp. BROWN SUGAR
1 EGG, lightly beaten
2 Tbsp. MELTED BUTTER

1/2 cup GOLD TEQUILA
1/4 cup MILK
1/2 tsp. grated ORANGE
   PEEL
1/2 cup PECANS, chopped

Mix all the ingredients together except pecans. The batter will be lumpy. Then stir in the pecans and fill lightly greased muffin tins 1/2 full. Bake at 400 degrees for 20 minutes. *Makes 12 muffins.*

APRICOT BREAD

Preheat oven to 350 degrees

1/4 cup GOLD TEQUILA
1 cup SUGAR
1/4 lb. BUTTER
2 EGGS, lightly beaten
1/2 cup ORANGE JUICE
2 cups all-purpose FLOUR
3 tsp. BAKING POWDER

1/2 tsp. SALT
1 tsp. grated ORANGE RIND
1 1/2 cups DRIED APRICOTS, chopped
1 Tbsp. all-purpose FLOUR
1 cup PECANS, chopped

Cream sugar and butter together, stir in eggs, orange juice, and tequila. Then add the two cups of flour, baking powder, salt and orange rind and beat until smooth. Coat the apricots with the tablespoon of flour and stir into the batter with the pecans. Spoon into a lightly greased 9 x 9 x 2 inch square pan and bake in a 350 degree oven for 45 minutes or until toothpick inserted in the center comes out clean. *Yield: 1 loaf.*

ORANGE PECAN BREAD

Preheat oven to 350 degrees

1/2 cup BUTTER
1 cup SUGAR
1/4 cup GOLD TEQUILA
1/2 cup ORANGE JUICE
1 Tbsp. ORANGE FLA- VORED LIQUEUR
1 EGG, lightly beaten

2 1/2 cups all-purpose FLOUR
3 tsp. BAKING POWDER
1 tsp. SALT
1/4 tsp. NUTMEG
1 tsp. grated ORANGE PEEL
1 cup PECANS, chopped

Cream together butter and sugar, stir in tequila, orange juice, orange liqueur and egg. Mix together flour, baking powder, salt, nutmeg, and orange peel and stir into the butter and sugar mixture. Add pecans and spoon batter into a lightly greased 9 x 5 x 3 inch loaf pan. Bake for 1 hour in a 350 degree oven or until a toothpick inserted in the center comes out clean. Remove from oven. Let stand for 5 - 6 minutes, remove from the pan and let cool on a wire rack. *Yield: 1 loaf.*

DESSERTS

There are many songs that celebrate tequila or in which tequila plays a walk-on or cameo role. "*La Que Se Fue*" is often played in Mexican cantinas and after the patrons wipe away the tears they order another round.

"La Que Se Fue"

Estoy en el rincon de una cantina,
Oyendo la cancion que yo pedi
Me estan sirviendo ahorita mi tequila,
Ya van mi pensamineto rumbo a ti.

Yo se que tu recuredo es mi desgracia
Y engo aqui nomas a recordar
Que amargas son las cosas que
nos pasan
Cuando hay una mujer que paga mal.

¿Quien no sabe en esta vida
La traicion tan conocida,
que nos deja un mal amor?
¿Quie no llega a la cantina,
Exigiendo su tequila y pidiendo
su cancion

Me estan sirviendo ya la del estribo
Ahorita ya no se si tento fe
Ahorita solamente yo les pido,
Que toque otra vez la *Que Se Fue*.
Yo lo que quiero es que vuelva, que
vuelva conmigo, laque se fue.

. . . and in English on
the following page . . .

APRICOT BALLS

1 pkg. (8 oz.) CREAM CHEESE
1 Tbsp. POWDERED SUGAR
1 cup DRIED APRICOTS
3/4 cup SWEETENED COCONUT FLAKES
1/2 cup PECANS
1 Tbsp. TEQUILA
1 Tbsp. TRIPLE SEC
1/2 tsp. grated ORANGE RIND
1/2 cup PECANS, finely chopped

Mix all the ingredients, except the finely chopped pecans, in a food processor with a steel blade. Roll the mixture into balls the size of a walnut, roll in the finely chopped pecans and chill until ready to serve. These are great served alongside a light pudding, flan or vanilla ice cream. *Yield: approximately 3 dozen.*

She Who Went Away

I'm in the corner of a cantina,
listening to the song I requested
They are just now serving my tequila,
Now my thoughts go toward you.

I know that your memory is my disgrace
And I come here only to remember.
How bitter are the things that happen to us
When there's an ungrateful woman.

Who in this life doesn't know
The betrayal so familiar, that is
left to us by a bad love?
Who doesn't come to the cantina,
Ordering his tequila and
requesting his song?

Now they're serving me one for the road,
Right now I don't know if I have faith
Right now I only ask them,
To play again *She Who Went Away*.
What I wish is that she return, return
with me, she who went away.

Printed with the permission of John F. Muir Publications; *The People's Guide to Mexico.*

TEQUILA CAKE

Although I often do cooking demonstrations I was completely surprised when I whipped up this cake for a large group at a university. When I finished the batter, there were gasps from the audience. It was the first time I ever received applause for a batter —but this cake is a show stopper!

Preheat oven to 325 degrees.

2 cups SUGAR
1 cup BUTTER
4 EGGS, lightly beaten
1 cup MILK
3 1/2 cups all-purpose FLOUR

3 tsp. BAKING POWDER
1/4 tsp. SALT
1/4 cup TEQUILA

Cream sugar, butter and eggs together. Stir in milk, then add the flour, baking powder, and salt and beat. Add the tequila and beat until smooth. The secret of this cake is to beat the batter very well until it becomes shiny.

Fold the batter into a greased and floured bundt pan. Bake for 1 hour in a 325 degree oven or until done when a toothpick inserted in the cake comes out clean. Cool cake on wire rack, then remove cake from pan, place on cake server or plate and top with the following **Tequila Cake Glaze.**

TEQUILA CAKE GLAZE

1 cup LIGHT BROWN SUGAR
1 cup DARK BROWN SUGAR
1/4 cup WATER

pinch SALT
1/4 cup TEQUILA
2 Tbsp. GRAND MARNIER

Place the sugars, water and salt in a saucepan and bring to a boil. Continue to cook until the mixture becomes semi-caramelized. Remove from heat, stir in the tequila and Grand Marnier and pour over the cake while glaze is still warm.

PEACH SHERBET

1 envelope UNFLAVORED GELATIN
1/2 cup TEQUILA
4 large, ripe PEACHES, pitted, peeled and sliced
1/2 cup LIGHT CORN SYRUP
1 cup MILK
1/2 cup PLAIN YOGURT
2 Tbsp. LEMON JUICE
MINT LEAVES

Dissolve gelatin in the tequila over low heat. Let cool and put in blender with the rest of the ingredients, except mint leaves, and blend. Pour in a 9 x 9 x 2 inch metal baking pan, cover with aluminum foil and freeze for at least 8 hours.

Remove from the freezer and let stand at room temperature for 10 minutes. Spoon in a large bowl and beat with an electric mixer at low speed until smooth but not melted. Pour into a mold and freeze for 4 hours or until firm.

When ready to serve, dip the mold in a small amount of hot water and unmold onto a cutting board. Slice the sherbet and make the following **Raspberry Sauce**. Spoon a thin layer of the sauce onto a dessert plate. Place a slice of sherbet on top of the sauce, garnish with fresh mint leaves and serve. *Serves 6 - 8.*

RASPBERRY SAUCE

1 cup RASPBERRIES
3/4 cup SUGAR or FRUCTOSE
3/4 cup TEQUILA
1 tsp. grated ORANGE PEEL

Put all the ingredients in a saucepan and bring to a boil, stirring occasionally to mash the berries. When the sugar has dissolved, let cool and strain. Chill the sauce in the refrigerator for at least 4 hours before serving. *Yield: approximately 2 cups.*

BANANA RELLENOS

3 ripe firm BANANAS,
    peeled and cut in half
    lengthwise
1/2 cup GOLD TEQUILA
1/2 cup ORANGE JUICE
1 Tbsp. LEMON JUICE

3 EGG WHITES
1/4 tsp. CREAM OF TARTAR
2 Tbsp. CORNSTARCH
2 Tbsp. all-purpose FLOUR
1/4 cup BUTTER
1/4 cup SUGAR or FRUCTOSE

Place bananas in a shallow dish, mix together tequila, orange juice, and lemon juice and pour over the bananas. Let stand for 1/2 hour. Beat egg whites until they start to form stiff peaks, add cream of tartar and continue beating until stiff. Mix cornstarch and flour together and fold into the egg whites.

Melt butter in a large non-stick frying pan, dip the bananas in the egg white batter and sauté until light brown. Remove to a warm platter. Stir the tequila orange mixture into the frying pan with the sugar and stir over medium heat until the sugar dissolves. Pour over the warm bananas, garnish with chocolate curls and serve at once. *Serves 6.*

FUNNEL CAKES

These are great fun to make and eat—especially with some hot chocolate on a cold winter's afternoon.

1 EGG, lightly beaten
1 cup MILK
2 Tbsp. SUGAR
1/2 tsp. SALT
1 tsp. BAKING POWDER
1 1/2 cups all-purpose FLOUR

1 Tbsp. TEQUILA
1/2 tsp. ground CARDAMON
1/2 tsp. ground NUTMEG
VEGETABLE OIL
POWDERED SUGAR

Mix all the ingredients (except oil and powdered sugar) together until smooth. Heat about 1 inch of vegetable oil in a heavy frying pan (I find cast iron works best). Pour the batter through a funnel in a random pattern of circles into the oil and fry until light brown and crispy. Drain, sprinkle generously with powdered sugar and serve warm. *Yields approximately 4 - 6 cakes.*

HEAVENLY
CHOCOLATE CAKE

Preheat oven to 375 degrees.

2 squares UNSWEETENED CHOCOLATE
1/4 cup BOILING WATER
1/4 cup TEQUILA
2 EGGS, well beaten
1 1/2 cups SUGAR
1/2 cup BUTTER, at room temperature
pinch SALT
1 tsp. VANILLA
3/4 cup BUTTERMILK
1 tsp. BAKING SODA
1 1/2 cups all-purpose FLOUR

Put chocolate, water and tequila in a saucepan and cook over low heat until chocolate is melted. Let cool, then stir the eggs into the chocolate mixture. Cream sugar and butter together and stir into the chocolate and egg mixture. Add salt, vanilla, buttermilk, baking soda and flour and stir until blended but do not over beat. Pour into 2 lightly greased and floured 8 inch round cake pans. Bake in a 375 degree oven for 45 minutes or until a toothpick comes out clean when inserted in the center. Let the cake cool in the pans on a wire rack. Remove from the pans and frost with **Tequila Frosting.**

TEQUILA FROSTING

1/2 cup BUTTER or MARGARINE, at room temperature
1/2 tsp. SALT
2 1/2 cups POWDERED SUGAR
1/2 tsp. VANILLA
1 Tbsp. GRAND MARNIER
3 - 4 Tbsp. TEQUILA

Cream butter, salt and sugar together. Add vanilla and Grand Marnier. Then slowly add tequila until the frosting is a spreadable consistency. Spread smoothly over cake.

LEMON SOUFFLÉ

Preheat oven to 375 degrees.

3 Tbsp. BUTTER
1/3 cup plus 1 Tbsp. SUGAR
3 Tbsp. all-purpose FLOUR
3/4 cup MILK
4 EGG YOLKS, well beaten

1 Tbsp. LEMON JUICE
1/4 cup TEQUILA
2 tsp. GRATED LEMON PEEL
4 EGG WHITES
1/2 tsp. CREAM OF TARTAR

Using 1 tablespoon of the butter grease the bottom and sides of a quart size soufflé dish and sprinkle 1 tablespoon of sugar over the butter. Mix the rest of the sugar, flour and milk together in a saucepan and cook until it comes to a boil and boil for 1 minute. Remove from the heat. Let cool then beat egg yolks into the mixture with a wire whisk. Add remaining 2 tablespoons of butter and return the pan to low heat and cook, stirring constantly, until the mixture thickens. Let cool slightly and stir in lemon juice, tequila and grated lemon peel. Beat egg whites until they start to form stiff peaks, add the cream of tartar and continue beating until stiff. Fold the egg whites into the cooled tequila mixture and pour into the prepared soufflé dish. Bake in a 375 degree oven for 45 minutes or until the soufflé has risen, is lightly brown and firm in the center. Serve at once with **Lemon Sauce**. *Serves 6.*

LEMON SAUCE

3 Tbsp. CORNSTARCH
3/4 cup TEQUILA
3/4 cup LEMON JUICE

1/2 cup SUGAR
1 Tbsp. BUTTER
1 tsp. LEMON PEEL, grated

Stir the cornstarch into the tequila until it dissolves, then put in the top of a double boiler with the sugar and butter, and cook over hot water for 10 minutes, stirring constantly. Then add the lemon juice, and lemon peel, and cook for 5 minutes, stirring until clear and warm. Serve warm with soufflé, bread puddings, or ginger bread. *Yield: approximately 2 cups.*

EL PASO PUMPKIN PIE

Preheat oven to 425 degrees.

2 EGGS, lightly beaten
1 can (16 oz.) solid pack PUMPKIN
3/4 cup SUGAR
1/2 tsp. SALT
1 tsp. ground CINNAMON
1/2 tsp. ground GINGER
1/4 tsp. ground CLOVES
1 1/2 cups EVAPORATED MILK
1 Tbsp. KAHLUA
2 Tbsp. TEQUILA
2 (9 inch) PIE CRUSTS

Thoroughly mix all ingredients together and pour into pie crusts. Bake in a 425 degree oven for 10 minutes. Reduce heat to 350 degrees and bake for an additional 45 minutes or until a toothpick inserted in the center of the pie comes out clean. Let cool to room temperature and serve garnished with **El Paso Pumpkin Pie Topping**. *Makes 2 pies.*

EL PASO
PUMPKIN PIE TOPPING

1/2 pint WHIPPING CREAM
2 Tbsp. SUGAR
1 Tbsp. KAHLUA

Whip cream until it starts to form peaks. Stir in sugar and kahlua and beat again until the cream forms stiff peaks. Serve a dollop of whipped cream on each piece of pie. Also excellent on bread puddings or pound cake.

CHOCOLATE TOPPED MARGARITA CHEESE CAKE

Preheat oven to 375 degrees.

CRUST:

1 3/4 cups GRAHAM CRACKER CRUMBS
1/4 cup WALNUTS, chopped
1 tsp. grated ORANGE PEEL
1/2 cup MELTED BUTTER

Mix all the ingredients together and press into the bottom and sides of a 9 inch springform pan.

FILLING:

3 EGGS, lightly beaten   **JUICE OF 1 LIME**
2 pkgs. (8 oz. each) CREAM   **2 Tbsp. TEQUILA**
**   CHEESE**   **1 Tbsp. TRIPLE SEC**
1 cup SUGAR   **3 cups SOUR CREAM**

Beat together eggs, cream cheese and sugar until smooth. Stir in lime juice, tequila, triple sec and sour cream until well blended.   Spoon into crust and bake in a 375 degree oven for 1 hour.   Turn off oven and let sit for 4 to 5 hours.   Then refrigerate for at least 6 hours before serving.

TOPPING:

1/2 cup BUTTER   **1 Tbsp. GOLD TEQUILA**
1/2 cup MILK   **sliced KIWIS**
1 cup POWDERED SUGAR   **RASPBERRIES**
1/4 cup COCOA   **MINT LEAVES**

Heat butter and milk in a microwave until butter has melted. Beat sugar and cocoa into milk mixture until smooth. Stir in tequila and then spread on top of the cheesecake. Refrigerate for 2 hours. Then layer kiwi slices around the edge of the cake, scatter raspberries across the top and place some mint leaves at strategic places for a very pleasing effect.

TEQUILA SHERBET

1 1/2 cups SUGAR
3 cups WATER
1/2 tsp. grated LIME PEEL
1/2 cup LIME JUICE
1/3 cup TEQUILA
1 EGG WHITE
1/4 tsp. coarse (Kosher) SALT

Bring sugar and water to a boil and cook for 5 minutes, stirring constantly. Stir in lime peel and cook for another minute. Remove from heat and stir in lime juice. Pour into metal freezing trays and place in freezer until the mixture thickens.

Take the sherbet out of the freezer and spoon it into a blender. Add tequila, egg white and salt and blend. Pour into the freezer tray and freeze until firm. *Serves 4.*

TEQUILA GRAPEFRUIT SHERBET

1/4 cup TEQUILA
1 envelope UNFLAVORED GELATIN
3 cups MILK
2 cups SUGAR
2 cups GRAPEFRUIT, peeled with the white
    membranes removed
1 cup PINK GRAPEFRUIT JUICE

Dissolve gelatin in the tequila in a saucepan, stir in milk and sugar and cook over low heat until the sugar dissolves. Put the grapefruit and grapefruit juice in a blender and blend until smooth. Add milk mixture and blend. Pour the mixture into an ice cream maker and process according to the manufacturer's direction. *Makes approximately 1 1/2 quarts.*

PECAN TART

Your favorite PASTRY recipe rolled out to 1/8 inch thick
3 cups PECAN HALVES
2   Tbsp. BUTTER
4 EGGS, lightly beaten
1/2 cup MAPLE SYRUP
1/2 cup LIGHT CORN SYRUP
1 cup SUGAR
1 Tbsp. TEQUILA
1 tsp. VANILLA

Place the pastry in a 10 1/2 inch tart pan with a removable bottom and refrigerate for 20 minutes. Arrange pecan halves in a circle on the chilled pastry. Melt butter and mix with the rest of the ingredients. Pour over pecans and bake in a 350 degree oven for 45 minutes or until the tart is set. Remove the sides of the tart pan and serve with the following **Dessert Cream**.

DESSERT CREAM

1/2 pint WHIPPING CREAM
2 Tbsp. SUGAR
1 tsp. TEQUILA
1 tsp. GRAND MARNIER

Beat whipping cream until it starts to stiffen, beat in sugar, tequila and Grand Marnier until the cream is stiff. Serve over tarts, ginger bread or any kind of fruit (especially good on strawberries!).

MANGO FLAMBÉ

All sorts of flambé dishes were once very popular in restaurants. I remember getting called out of the kitchen many a day when an inexperienced waiter couldn't get a dish to flame. The trick, of course, is to have the liqueur slightly warm before trying to ignite.

If you don't have the burners and set up to do this tableside you can do this dish in the kitchen. Have the ice cream ready—and carry the pan to your waiting and expectant guests.

4 serving bowls FRENCH VANILLA ICE CREAM
1/8 lb. BUTTER
1/4 cup POWDERED SUGAR
1 Tbsp. LEMON JUICE
1 large MANGO, peeled, pitted and sliced
1/2 cup TEQUILA

Spoon the ice cream into the bowls and put on the table.

Melt butter in a copper frying pan or sauté pan. Stir in sugar and lemon juice. Add mango slices and gently spoon the liquid over them and cook for 4 - 5 minutes. Heat the tequila until just warm, pour over the mango slices, ignite it with a match and spoon the mangoes and sauce over the ice cream. *Serves 4.*

FRUIT A LA FORMENTERA

1 medium sized CANTALOUPE, peeled and cut into cubes
1 cup RASPBERRIES
1/4 cup TEQUILA
2 Tbsp. TRIPLE SEC
8 oz. PEACH FLAVORED YOGURT
1/2 cup PEANUTS, run through a food chopper

Place the cantaloupe and raspberries in a glass bowl, pour the tequila and triple sec over them, stir gently, cover and chill in the refrigerator for 1 hour. Remove from the refrigerator and spoon into 4 dessert glasses or plates. Top with the yogurt, sprinkle the nuts on top and serve. *Serves 4.*

ORANGE BISCOTTI

The addition of orange juice and tequila to this classic Italian cookie makes this a perfect pastry to serve with after dinner coffee or at teatime.

1 cup SUGAR
1/2 cup BUTTER, at
   room temperature
2 EGGS, lightly beaten
2 Tbsp. TEQUILA
2 Tbsp. ORANGE JUICE
1 tsp. grated ORANGE PEEL

2 1/2 cups all-purpose
   FLOUR
2 tsp. BAKING POWDER
1/4 tsp. SALT
1/3 cup SLIVERED
   ALMONDS

Mix sugar and butter together, then add eggs, tequila, orange juice, orange peel and beat. Stir in flour, baking powder and salt. Then stir in the almonds. Place the mixture on a lightly floured pastry board and knead until the dough makes a ball—approximately 5 - 6 minutes. Divide dough into two halves and roll the halves into a rope about the length of a cookie sheet. Place each rope on an ungreased cooking sheet and bake in a 325 degree oven for 20 to 30 minutes or until golden brown. Remove from the baking sheet and let cool for 6 - 7 minutes. Slice diagonally to 1/2 inch pieces, lay the pieces flat on the cookie sheet and bake in a 325 degree oven for 5 minutes. Turn over and bake for 5 more minutes. Let cool to room temperature and store in a covered container. *Makes approximately 3 dozen.*

Who was Margarita?

*Margarita was her name
And the drink named after her
Ensured her lasting fame.*

*Just who was this damsel fair
Whose face and figure prompted
A bartender to create a drink with care?*

*Was she an actress out on the town,
A demure señorita flirting coyly,
Or a dedicated drinker slugging tequila down?*

*To this day the mystery remains
But as we lift our frosted glasses aloft
We salute her just the same!*

MARGARITA PIE

CRUST:

1 1/2 cups CHOCOLATE WAFER CRUMBS
1/4 lb. BUTTER or MARGARINE
1/2 cup WALNUTS, ground

Melt the butter or margarine, mix with the chocolate wafer crumbs and ground walnuts and press into the bottom and sides of a 9 inch pie pan.

FILLING:

1/4 cup LEMON JUICE
1/3 cup LIME JUICE
1 Tbsp. TRIPLE SEC
1 Tbsp. TEQUILA
1/2 tsp. SALT
1 can (14 oz.) CONDENSED MILK

1 tsp. grated LIME PEEL
1 container (8 oz.)
WHIPPED TOPPING
SWEETENED CHOCOLATE
CURLS

Beat lemon juice, lime juice, triple sec, tequila and salt into the condensed milk. Stir in lime peel, fold in whipped topping and spoon into prepared chocolate crust. Refrigerate for at least two hours before servings. Garnish with chocolate curls and serve. *Yield: 8 servings.*

CHOCOLATE FONDUE

1 lb. MILK CHOCOLATE
1 cup WHIPPING CREAM
3 Tbsp. TEQUILA

1 Tbsp. ORANGE FLAVORED
LIQUEUR

Break chocolate into pieces and place in a saucepan. Add cream and melt chocolate over low heat, stirring constantly. When chocolate has melted into the cream, add tequila and orange flavored liqueur and cook over low heat until all the ingredients are well blended. Pour into a fondue pot and place the pot over a low flame.

Serve with fresh strawberries, fresh pineapple, sliced apples, sliced pears or pretzels for everyone to dip into the chocolate. *Serves 4 - 6.*

BEVERAGES

Variations on Drinking Tequila

Some people lick the fleshy part on the back of their hand between their thumb and index finger, sprinkle on salt, take a drink of tequila from a shot glass, lick off salt, then bite into a piece of lime. Other folks lick the salt before taking a drink and yet others get right down to drinking the tequila first, then finishing the ritual with the salt and lime. Although I've been told it's not at all correct, I have seen patrons at bars squeeze the lime onto the same part of their hand, sprinkle on the salt, lick their hand and then slug back the tequila.

Another variation on this theme is called "slamming" and includes going through the lime and salt ritual, then knocking back an entire shot of tequila at once—usually in an extra tall (4 to 5 inch) shot glass—then slamming the glass on the table or bar.

Other serious tequila drinkers down what is called a "depth charge", where they sink a shot glass of tequila into a three quarters full glass of beer and then drink it. I've never tried it since I have both poor motor control and soft tooth enamel.

MARVELOUS MARGARITAS

*Having tried many different ways to make margaritas, this recipe
with fresh lime juice gets rave reviews every time we serve it.*

5 oz. WHITE TEQUILA
4 oz. TRIPLE SEC
2 oz. FRESH LIME JUICE
coarse (Kosher) SALT
THIN LIME SLICES

Pour the tequila, triple sec and lime juice in a blender with ice
and blend until smooth.   Wet your finger with a little triple sec and
rub the liqueur around the top of 2 large wine or cocktail glasses.
Place the salt on a small plate and twist the rim of the glass on the
salt to coat the rim.   Pour in the margaritas, garnish with lime slices
and serve. *Serves 2.*

TEQUILA MARY

1 1/2 oz. TEQUILA
1 cup TOMATO JUICE
1 Tbsp. GREEN CHILE, such as Anaheim, chopped
5 - 6 ICE CUBES

Put all the ingredients in a blender and blend until smooth.
Pour into a large stemmed glass and serve with a rib of celery or
a pickled jalapeño as garnish. *Serves 1.*

PINK CADILLAC

1 1/2 oz. TEQUILA GOLD
1/2 oz. TRIPLE SEC
1/2 oz. LEMON JUICE
1 cup CRANBERRY JUICE
CLUB SODA

Pour tequila, triple sec, lemon juice and cranberry juice over
ice in a tall highball glass.   Stir well, top with club soda and serve
with a slice of lemon or lime. *Serves 1.*

WARM ME HEART

6 cups APPLE CIDER
1 CINNAMON STICK
1/2 tsp. ground NUTMEG
1/2 tsp. ground ALLSPICE
1/4 tsp. ground CINNAMON
1 tsp. grated ORANGE RIND
4 oz. TEQUILA

Pour apple cider in a saucepan. Put the cinnamon stick, nutmeg, allspice, cinnamon and orange rind in a spice bag or tie in a clean piece of cloth such as cheese cloth and place in the cider. Heat over low heat for 30 minutes. Pour the tequila equally into 4 heavy glasses or mugs, top with the cider and serve. *Serves 4.*

TEQUILA PUNCH

1 quart PINEAPPLE SHERBET
1 can (6 oz.) frozen PINK
    LEMONADE CONCENTRATE
2 cups TEQUILA
2 bottles (2 liters each) 7-UP® or
    other LIME-BASED SODA
MINT LEAVES

Put the sherbet in the bottom of a punch bowl. Mix lemonade and tequila together and pour over the sherbet. Top with the lime soda, garnish with mint leaves and orange slices and serve. *Serves 24.*

CARO MIO COCKTAIL

1 oz. TEQUILA
1/2 oz. GALLIANO
1/2 cup ORANGE JUICE
ORANGE SLICE

Pour tequila, Galliano, and orange juice into a blender, add ice and blend. Serve in a stemmed glass with orange slice. *Serves 1.*

LAKE CHAPALA COCKTAIL

A friend of ours spent some time in Lake Chapala, a popular Mexican resort for American retirees. He gave us this recipe and said, "We had lots of time on our hands and decided to see which one of us could come up with the best tequila drink. This is mine, and I think I won hands down."

6 SUGAR CUBES
12 drops AROMATIC BITTERS
6 oz. WHITE TEQUILA

1 bottle CHAMPAGNE
THINLY SLICED LEMON

Place one cube of sugar in the bottom of each champagne glass. Shake a couple drops of bitters over the sugar cube and crush the cube with the back of a spoon. Pour 1 ounce of tequila into each glass, top with champagne, garnish with thinly sliced lemon and serve. *Serves 6.*

SIGNATURE TEQUILA SUNRISE

A friend brought some out-of-town visitors by the office to buy one of my books. I offered to autograph it for them—but they would rather have, they said, one of my famous special tequila sunrises. Hence the name.

1 oz. TEQUILA
1/4 cup ORANGE JUICE
1/2 oz. TRIPLE SEC

1/4 oz. GRENADINE
ORANGE SLICE

Place tequila, orange juice, triple sec and grenadine in a blender with ice and blend. Serve in a stemmed glass garnished with a slice of orange. *Serves 1.*

ROCKY POINT BLOODY MARY

I developed this version of the Bloody Mary on one of our many trips to Puerto Peñasco (Rocky Point). It's great served with brunch!

8 oz. WHITE TEQUILA
4 tsp. LEMON JUICE
1 cup CLAM JUICE
2 cups TOMATO JUICE
8 - 12 dashes TABASCO®
8 dashes WORCESTERSHIRE SAUCE

1/2 tsp. SALT
1/4 tsp. coarse ground
   BLACK PEPPER
1/4 tsp. CELERY SALT
4 LEMON SLICES

    In a pitcher mix together tequila, lemon juice, clam juice, tomato juice, Tabasco and Worcestershire sauce. Add salt, pepper, and celery salt. Fill four tall glasses with ice cubes. Pour the mixture over the ice, garnish with lemon slices and serve. *Serves 4.*

NOGALES ALICE LEMONADE

A long ago friend named Alice loved tequila, but she didn't want her friends and relatives to think she was drinking alcohol so she came up with this lemonade that looked innocent enough sitting on her patio table in case company dropped by.

JUICE OF 2 large
   LEMONS
4 cups WATER

3 jiggers (3 oz.) TEQUILA
4 Tbsp. SUGAR
   (or more to taste)

    Mix all ingredients together in a pitcher, add ice and stir. *Makes 2 tall drinks.*

SUITS-ME-TO-A-TEA

I'm an ardent tea drinker and on those special, cold afternoons when you want the extra warmth of liquor this makes a lovely sipping drink.

1 oz. TEQUILA
1 oz. GRAND MARNIER

1 cup HOT SPICED TEA
Slice of ORANGE

    Pour tequila and Grand Marnier into a heavy mug or glass. Add hot tea and stir. Garnish with an orange slice. *Serves 1.*

BLUE LAGOON COCKTAIL

1 oz. TEQUILA
1 oz. BLUE CURACAO
1/2 cup LEMONADE
Sprig of MINT

Fill a highball glass with ice, and pour the tequila, curacao and lemonade over the ice and stir. Serve with sprig of mint. *Serves 1.*

PIÑA COCKTAIL

1 oz. TEQUILA
1/2 cup PINEAPPLE JUICE
1/2 oz. LIME JUICE
THIN LIME SLICE

Pour all the ingredients into a blender with ice and blend until smooth. Serve in a cocktail glass with a lime slice. *Serves 1.*

VIVA VERONICA

5 oz. TEQUILA
1 oz. LIME JUICE
1 oz. CHERRY BRANDY
LIME SLICES

Pour the tequila, lime juice and brandy into a blender with ice and blend. Serve garnished with a lime slice. *Serves 2.*

LA PAZ COCKTAIL

1 oz. TEQUILA
1 oz. CREAM OF COCONUT
2 oz. ORANGE JUICE

Pour all the ingredients in a blender with ice and blend until smooth. *Serves 1.*

TECOLOTE ROSA

This translates into English as "the pink owl" and its bittersweet taste is especially refreshing on a hot summer day.

1 oz. TEQUILA
1/2 oz. SWEET VERMOUTH
1/2 oz. CAMPARI
CLUB SODA
LEMON SLICE

Pour tequila, vermouth and Campari over ice in a tall glass. Add club soda to fill. Stir and top with a lemon slice and serve. *Serves 1.*

TEQUILA BRANDY

I liter TEQUILA, with 1 cup poured off
3/4 cup SUGAR
1/2 cup ORANGE JUICE
RIND of ONE ORANGE

Mix tequila, sugar and orange juice together. Poke the orange rind into the tequila bottle, pour the tequila mixture back into the bottle, shake until the sugar is dissolved. Remove the orange peel after 2 weeks. Great as an after dinner drink, or serve with ice and club soda as a cocktail. *Yield: 1 liter.*

HOLA COCKTAIL

"Hola" is Spanish for "hello" and this cocktail not only says hello but "How are you? Hope you're having a good time" . . . You fill in the rest.

1 oz. COCONUT MILK
1 oz. TRIPLE SEC
2 oz. GOLD TEQUILA
1/4 cup CREAM

Pour everything into a blender and blend with ice until smooth and pour into a cocktail glass. *Serves 1.*

CLOUD NINE COCKTAIL

The noted artist and photographer, Daniel Zolinsky, recently returned from a stint in Greece where he was shooting photos for his latest book. Living in the Southwest he is accustomed to seeing tequila in most drinking establishments. However, he was taken aback when he walked into the Argo Bar on the island of Sifnos to find it stocked with a large array of different brands of tequila.

The owner was extremely proud of his tequila concoctions and asked Daniel to try this one. When he heard I was writing this book he passed the recipe on to me.

1 1/2 oz. KAHLUA
1 Tbsp. WHIPPING CREAM
1 oz. TEQUILA

    Fill the bottom of a lowball glass with Kahlua, drop the whipping cream from a spoon onto the liqueur, then pour the tequila on top of the cream. Do not stir. *Serves 1.*

FROZEN MANGO-TEQUILA FLIP

2 cups RIPE MANGOES
4 Tbsp. LIME JUICE
4 Tbsp. SUGAR
8 Tbsp. TEQUILA
4 cups CRUSHED ICE
MINT LEAVES

    Place all the ingredients in a blender and blend until smooth. Pour into large wine glasses, garnish with mint leaves and serve. *Serves 4.*

RASPBERRY-TEQUILA COFFEE

1 oz. TEQUILA
1 oz. RASPBERRY LIQUEUR
COFFEE

Pour tequila and raspberry liqueur in the bottom of a large mug or heavy glass. Pour in coffee and stir. Top with whipped cream* and serve. *Serves 1.*

* You can fold a small amount of raspberry syrup or raspberry all-fruit preserves into the whipped cream for a sweeter taste and an elegant pink color.

CAFÉ MEXICANO

1 oz. TEQUILA   **1/2 tsp. SUGAR**
1/2 oz. KAHLUA   **COFFEE**
1/4 tsp. ground CINNAMON **WHIPPED CREAM**

Pour tequila and Kahlua into a large mug or heavy glass, stir in cinnamon and sugar, pour in the coffee, top with whipped cream and serve. *Serves 1.*

CAFÉ CARAMBA

1 oz. TEQUILA   **3/4 cup BLACK COFFEE**
1 tsp. TRIPLE SEC   **LIME PEEL**
1 tsp. SUGAR

Pour tequila and triple sec in a mug or heavy glass. Stir in the sugar, add the coffee, garnish with a lime peel and serve hot. *Serves 1.*

KISSING THE BLARNEY STONE

This drink is great to celebrate St. Patrick's Day although one too many and you may just want to kiss everybody in sight.

1 1/2 oz. TEQUILA
1 oz. BAILEY'S IRISH CREAM WHISKEY
COFFEE
WHIPPED CREAM
GREEN MARASCHINO CHERRY

Pour tequila and Bailey's into a large mug or heavy glass. Add coffee and stir. Top with whipped cream and garnish with a green maraschino cherry. *Serves 1.*

ICED CHOCOLATE-TEQUILA COFFEE

Use half the amount of your regular coffee blend mixed with half Dutch Chocolate Coffee blend. Brew as you normally would for 8 cups. Let cool.

For each glass served - fill glass with ice then add:

1 oz. TEQUILA
1/2 oz. KAHLUA
ORANGE SLICES

Pour in the cold coffee. Garnish with orange slices. *Serves 1.*

MY KINDA COCOA

This is strictly an adult drink for those cold winter nights when coffee won't do—and chocolate will.

1 Tbsp. COCOA	**1 oz. KAHLUA**
3 tsp. SUGAR	**1 cup HOT MILK**
1 oz. TEQUILA	**WHIPPED CREAM**

Spoon the cocoa and sugar into the bottom of a large mug or heavy glass. Stir in tequila and Kahlua, pour in the hot milk and stir well. Top with a dollop of whipped cream and serve. *Serves 1.*

Index

Meet the Author

Lynn Nusom has owned and operated award winning restaurants and was the executive chef of a four-star four-diamond hotel. He has written over 700 newspaper and magazine articles on food, reviews cookbooks, makes frequent appearances on television demonstrating cooking techniques and gives lectures on southwestern cuisine.

Lynn Nusom is the author of eight cook books: *The New Mexico Cook Book, The Tequila Cook Book, The Sizzling Southwestern Cookbook, Christmas in New Mexico, Christmas in Arizona, Cooking in the Land of Enchantment, Spoon Desserts; Custards, Cremes and Elegant Fruit Desserts,* and *The Billy-The-Kid Cookbook.*

The author makes his home in southern New Mexico with his wife, Guylyn Morris Nusom.

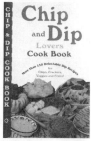

ORDER BLANK

GOLDEN WEST PUBLISHERS

☼ 4113 N. Longview Ave. • Phoenix, AZ 85014

www.goldenwestpublishers.com • **1-800-658-5830** • FAX 602-279-6901

Qty	Title	Price	Amount
	Arizona Cook Book	**5.95**	
	Best Barbecue Recipes	**5.95**	
	Chip and Dip Cook Book	**5.95**	
	Chili-Lovers' Cook Book	**5.95**	
	Christmas in Arizona Cook Book	**9.95**	
	Christmas in New Mexico Cook Book	**9.95**	
	Cowboy Cartoon Cook Book	**7.95**	
	Easy Recipes for Wild Game & Fish	**6.95**	
	Gourmet Gringo Cook Book	**14.95**	
	Mexican Desserts & Drinks	**6.95**	
	Mexican Family Favorites Cook Book	**6.95**	
	New Mexico Cook Book	**5.95**	
	Quick-n-Easy Mexican Recipes	**5.95**	
	Real New Mexico Chile Cook Book	**6.95**	
	Salsa Lovers Cook Book	**5.95**	
	Take This Chile & Stuff It!	**6.95**	
	Tequila Cook Book	**7.95**	
	Texas Cook Book	**5.95**	
	Tortilla Lovers Cook Book	**6.95**	
	Wholly Frijoles! The Whole Bean Cook Book	**6.95**	
Shipping & Handling Add ▦➡	U.S. & Canada	$3.00	
	Other countries	$5.00	

☐ My Check or Money Order Enclosed $

☐ MasterCard ☐ VISA ($20 credit card minimum)

(Payable in U.S. funds)

Acct. No.	Exp. Date
Signature	
Name	Telephone
Address	
City/State/Zip **Call for a FREE catalog of all of our titles**	Tequila Ck. Bk.
7/00	

This order blank may be photo-copied.